A Comprehensive Guide to Life,
Money and Social Success

# *Essential Life Skills for Teens 2023*

approved by teens

with exercises

## Cristina L. Turingray

# CONTENTS

# *Chapter 1: Introduction*

**Raising Three: A Glimpse into My Learnings.**

I've got three kids, so I've seen firsthand the rollercoaster of the teen years. I dream big for them: awesome careers, great friends, and being their best selves. But let's face it, being a teen isn't always a walk in the park.

**This Book? It's Your Compass ✳**

1. **Decoding Parents**: Ever wondered why parents say or want certain things? We'll break it down.
2. **Why Bother?**: It's not just about making parents happy. These tips and tricks can seriously benefit YOU.
3. **Life Skills, Unlocked**: Learn simple strategies to navigate challenges, and maybe, just maybe, get your folks to chill a bit.

**Not Just Words, We've Got Activities! 🎨**

This isn't a dull textbook. We've sprinkled in cool exercises and interesting tidbits to keep things lively.

**To The Point 🎯**

No endless lectures here. We're keeping it straightforward, offering you real insights for real situations.

Ready to get started? Let's make the most of these transformative years!

# Chapter 2: Skills and How to Nail Them

## The Powerhouse Skill: Mastering the Art of Learning 🎓

Ever heard the saying, "Give a person a fish, and you feed them for a day; teach them how to fish, and you feed them for a lifetime"? The idea here is simple: knowing how to learn is like having a superpower. It's the backbone of every skill, talent, and hobby you'll ever pick up. In a world that's changing every second, being able to adapt and learn new things? That's golden.

## Breaking Down Skills ⚙️

A skill is like a puzzle. At first, it seems complex and confusing. But piece by piece, with time and practice, it all comes together. Remember when you first tried riding a bike or playing an instrument? It was challenging, but the more you did it, the better you got.

## Repetition: The Secret Sauce 🔁

Here's the magic formula:

**Understanding**: Try something three times, and you'll start to get the hang of it.
**Mastery**: Want to nail it? Repeat at least ten times. Practice doesn't just make perfect, it builds confidence.

## Digging for Resources

Your journey to pick up new skills is backed by amazing tools:

**Consult the Wizards**: Every field has its pros. Don't be shy – ask them questions!

**Google's Goldmine**: The web is bursting with guides and articles. Dive in!

**Video Vibes on YouTube**: Watching someone do it can sometimes be the best lesson. Find a tutorial that clicks with you.

**ChatBots to the Rescue**: Platforms like ChatGPT are always here. Stuck or curious? Just hit it up.

So, gear up! The universe of skills is expansive and thrilling. All it takes is a dash of curiosity and a sprinkle of persistence. Let's do this! 🚀 💥

## *Persistence: The Power Trait* 💪

Ever met someone who just doesn't give up, no matter how tough things get? That trait, my friend, is called persistence, and it's pretty much a superpower. Embrace it, wear it proudly, and never let anyone make you doubt it.

### The Alibaba Journey: Meet Jack Ma 📖

Ever heard of Alibaba, the e-commerce giant? Well, its founder, Jack Ma, has a story that's all about persistence. He faced numerous setbacks:

- Rejected from 30 jobs, including one at KFC where 24 out of 25 applicants got hired (yes, he was the only one left out).
- Failed twice in college entrance exams.
- His online ventures before Alibaba didn't succeed.

Despite the universe seemingly against him, Jack Ma didn't quit. He believed in the potential of the internet economy in China. Gathering a small team in his apartment, he launched Alibaba. And with perseverance and an undying spirit, he turned Alibaba into a global e-commerce behemoth. Moral of the story? Never underestimate the power of not giving up.

## Complex Task? Break It Down! 📦

Facing something that feels like climbing Mount Everest? Don't stress! Slice that mountain into smaller hills. Tackle one bit at a time. And remember, every step you take? That already makes you pretty awesome.

## Questions are Cool 😎

Not getting something? Just ask! Asking isn't a sign of ignorance. In fact, it's the exact opposite. It shows you're keen to learn and grow. Remember: The only silly question is the one that's never asked.

## Your Potential? Sky's the Limit! 🚀

Here's the deal: You can achieve anything you set your mind to. Sure, sometimes it might take a little longer than expected. But armed with patience and persistence, there's no dream too big.

Embrace the journey, cherish the learning, and remember: you've got what it takes! 💥

# Chapter 3: The Secret Art of Tidying (Easy Way)

## *Cleaning Up: For Your Peace and Theirs* 🧹

Let's face it, cleaning might not be your favorite pastime. But, if a few quick moves can make your space look great and give you a break from parent-nagging? Why not?

**Mastering the Clear Surfaces Rule**

Clear surfaces are your best friends when you want a room to *appear* tidier than it might be. Here's a quick checklist for you:

1. **Desk Area**:
   What to Keep: Stationery items, laptop, a notebook.

Clear Out: Random papers, yesterday's snacks, and that cup from three days ago.

## 2. **Bed**:
   What to Keep: Pillows, a blanket or two, maybe a stuffed animal if that's your jam.
   Clear Out: Clothes, books, and whatever you pulled out from your closet and didn't wear.

## 3. **Nightstand**:
   What to Keep: A lamp, maybe a book or your phone charger.
   Clear Out: Empty water bottles, candy wrappers, and other knick-knacks.

## 4. **Dresser or Shelves**:
   What to Keep: Some decor, perhaps a few favorite items on display.
   Clear Out: Random clutter, items that don't belong, and stuff you haven't used or admired in a month.

## 5. **Floor**:
   What to Keep: Honestly? Nothing. Maybe a rug.
   Clear Out: Shoes, backpacks, and whatever else decided to make the floor its home.

The idea? Keep only the essentials in sight and find a home for everything else. Even if you're just shoving it into a drawer for now (we won't tell).

A few minutes spent on this, and voila! A room that's parent-approved (mostly) and still chill enough for you. Cheers to smart, lazy cleaning! 🧹 🥂

# *Floors: The Forgotten Frontier*

## Sweeping & Mopping: Making Floors Shine! ❄️

Alright, a clear floor is fantastic, but let's not forget about that sneaky layer of dust or the occasional spills. Here's how to get your floors sparkling with a broom and mop combo!

## Step 1: Sweeping Basics 🖌️

1. **Choose Your Weapon**: For indoors, a broom with fine bristles is your best friend. They pick up the smaller dust particles that thicker bristles might miss.

2. **Proper Grip**: Stand straight, one hand near the top and the other halfway down the broom handle. This stance gives control and eases the back.

3. **The Technique**: Use short strokes, always sweeping in one direction, preferably towards you. Focus especially on corners and baseboards, where sneaky dirt loves to hang out.

4. **Gather Up**: Once all the dirt's in one place, it's dustpan time. Get all that dust and dirt scooped up and thrown away.

## Step 2: Mopping 101

1. **Pick the Right Mop**: There are many types out there. The string mop is classic and great for deeper cleans. Flat mops are easier to maneuver and are great for a quick once-over.

2. **Prepare Your Water**: Fill a bucket with warm water. Add a dash of floor cleaner, following the label's instructions. No floor cleaner? A bit of mild dish soap will do in a pinch.

3. **Wring it Out**: Dunk the mop into your soapy water, ensuring the mop head is fully saturated. But before hitting the floor, wring out any excess water. You want the mop damp, not dripping.

4. **Start Mopping**: Begin at the farthest corner of the room and work your way towards the door. Use a figure-eight or S-pattern to cover the surface without pushing dirt around.

5. **Rinse & Repeat**: If your mop water gets super dirty, dump it, remix, and continue. Your floor deserves clean water!

6. **Dry and Done**: Once you're done mopping, allow the floor to air dry. To speed things up, you can open a window or use a fan. Make sure the floor is completely dry before walking on it to prevent slips.

With these steps, not only will your floor look clean, but it'll also have that fresh feel underfoot, and a nice shine to boot. Plus, next time you sprawl on the floor for a gaming session or an impromptu dance break, it'll be on a spotless surface. Talk about leveling up your room game! 🎮🕺📼

## Try the 15-Minute Daily Boost 🚀

### Why 15 Minutes? 🕐

Sounds too good to be true, right? Can you really make a dent in room cleanliness in just a quarter of an hour? Absolutely!

Consistency trumps long, exhausting cleaning sessions any day. By giving just 15 minutes daily, you build a habit, keep messes in check, and believe it or not, free up your weekends from those marathon cleaning sessions.

**Here's How to Rock Those 15 Minutes:**

1. **Set a Timer** ⏰: Seriously, do it. It's way easier to convince yourself to start when you know there's a clear end in sight. Plus, it turns cleaning into a fun, beat-the-clock game.

2. **Priority Zones** 🎯: Identify the "mess hotspots" in your room. Maybe it's your desk, your bedside table, or that infamous chair everyone dumps clothes on. Start there.

3. **Surface Swipe** 🧽: Spend a couple of minutes wiping down surfaces. A quick dust or wipe can make a world of difference.

4. **Ground Patrol** 👟: Ensure there's a clear path in your room. Pick up anything that doesn't belong on the floor. If you did our earlier steps, this should be a breeze!

5. **Daily Ditch** 🗑: Challenge yourself to find one thing every day you can toss out or donate. Old receipts, that shirt you haven't worn in a year – it adds up!

6. **Final Touches** ✨: Maybe straighten up your bedspread, align your shoes, or give your room a quick spritz of a pleasant scent. These tiny gestures elevate the vibe.

Do this daily, and you'll be amazed at how your room transforms. And the best part? You barely feel the effort, and yet, the benefits are HUGE.

In a month, you won't just have a cleaner space; you'll have developed a priceless habit that can apply to other parts of your life too. Because when you take control of your space, even just 15 minutes at a time, you take control of your mindset. And that's a total win! 🎇 🏆 🎊

## *Decoding Parent Expectations & Planning Your Move: The Big List vs. The Small List*

Parents often have a mountain of expectations, but when it comes to room tidiness, those expectations can generally be divided into two categories:

1. **The Big List**: These are the major things parents usually harp on about. They want these done, let's say, once a week. It might include tasks like:
     - A full room cleaning, including vacuuming/mopping.
     - Changing and washing your bed linens.
     - Deep cleaning and organizing your desk or study space.

2. **The Small List**: The everyday things. They're small but do them daily, and you'll reduce the chance of hearing the "Your room's a mess!" speech. Things like:
     - Making your bed.
     - Picking up clothes.
     - Clearing any dishes or trash.

Understanding these lists and their importance in your parents' minds can help you address their concerns without getting overwhelmed.

**Planning Your Daily & Weekly Actions**:

1. **Daily Dose of Tidiness**:
   - Set a regular time: Maybe right after waking up, you make your bed, or before sleeping, you ensure all clothes are in their place.
   - Use the 15-minute boost (as discussed earlier) to maintain the Small List items and avoid the build-up of mess.

2. **The Weekly Wonder**:
   - Choose a day: Maybe Saturday morning or Sunday evening, whatever fits your schedule. This is when you tackle the Big List.
   - Break it down: Don't aim to do everything at once. Vacuum first, take a break, then maybe organize your closet.
   - Reward yourself: After a successful clean-up session, do something you love. Maybe a treat, a game, or watching your favorite show. It makes the task something to look forward to!

Remember, tidying isn't about impressing your parents or avoiding their nagging (though, let's be real, that's a nice perk). It's about creating a space where you can chill, study, and hang out without feeling cluttered or stressed. Plus, mastering this skill now will set you up for success when you have your own place! 🏠 🛸 🎸

Alright, I'll restructure it with a more logical flow, starting with the "why", then moving to the "how" of paper, followed by the phone.

## *Quick Challenge: The 3-Item Quest!* 💥

**Goal**: To get a quick win and make a tiny but impactful change in your space.

**Time**: Just 5 minutes. Yep, you can probably finish even faster than your favorite TikTok dance!

**Instructions**:

1. **Stand Up and Stretch** 🧍: Take a moment. Look around your room. Feel its vibe.

2. **Spot & Identify** 👀: Find three things in your room that aren't in their proper place. Maybe it's a hoodie on the floor, a book out of its shelf, or your headphones sprawled on your bed.

3. **Move & Groove** 👋: Put each of those items where they belong. Dance, slide, hop, or moonwalk your way to doing it - make it fun!

4. **Pause & Feel** ♡: Take a deep breath. Look around again. How does your room feel now with just those three things in order? A bit better, right?

5. **Pat Yourself on the Back** 🎉: Small steps lead to big results. You've just taken a step!

Remember, every item in its right place contributes to a more harmonious and organized space. And starting with just three can create a ripple effect. So, whenever your room feels a tad chaotic, think of this 3-item quest and go on a mini-adventure. Happy tidying! 🌈 🚀

# Chapter 4: Time Management: The Ultimate Life Hack ⏱️🎮

**Intro**: Alright, let's get real. We all wish days had more than 24 hours. But what if I told you that you can *feel* like they do? Welcome to the game of Time Management, where you level up, get more freedom, and make your life way cooler.

## Unlocking Planning Skills:

1. **Epic Planning**:
   - 📆 **Event Calendar**: Plot out the big boss battles, like exams or projects. Prep in advance and defeat them with ease.
   - 💥 **Skill Tree Goals**: What do you want to unlock this month? A new hobby? A new game? Plan it!

## 2. **Weekly Raids**:

- 📋 **Quest Lists**: Line up the week's adventures. What dungeons will you explore? Which tasks will you conquer?
- ⧗ **Time Portals**: Decide when you'll tackle each quest. Maybe afternoons are for school missions, evenings for gaming.

## 3. **Daily Side Quests**:

- ✅ **Adventure Checklist**: Every morning, pick your challenges for the day. The sweetest win? Checking them off.
- 🥇 **Daily Trophies**: Out of your list, pick 3 epic wins for the day. Nail them, and you're a legend.

Benefits for You:
- 🎉 **More Free Time**: Get stuff done faster, and guess what? More time to game, chill, or hang out.
- 🎮 **Less Stress During Game Time**: With your tasks done, you can game guilt-free!
- 👾 **Level Up in Real Life**: Get better grades, more free time, and prove you can juggle it all.


## *Unleashing the Power of Paper and Phone*

Okay, let's keep it real. Time management isn't just about being "organized." It's about maximizing fun, reducing stress, and getting more YOU-time. The better you manage, the more epic things you can fit in!

**Paper Planning: The Classic Strategy**:

1. **The Charm of Lists**:

📋 **See It, Do It**: Write down your daily tasks. Visual reminders = things actually getting done. Plus, crossing stuff off feels like winning a mini-game.

### 2. Mind Maps: Unlock Your Next Move:

🌐 Diving into a project? Sketch it out. It's like drawing a game plan. See the big picture, break down levels, and tackle 'em one by one.

### 3. Sticky Note Alerts:

🏹 Colorful, in-your-face reminders. Place them around – your desk, books, or even your door. Perfect for stuff that just can't wait!

### Phone Planning: Leveling Up Your Game:

### 1. Timely Nudges:

⏰ Alarms aren't just wake-up calls. Use them for homework reminders, gaming breaks, or that online concert you can't miss.

### 2. Dive into Digital:

🗂 There are rad apps designed to keep you on track. Explore apps like "Trello", "Todoist", or "Notion" to set goals and smash 'em.

🍅 And for focus? The "Pomodoro Technique" through apps like "Forest" lets you work in short, effective bursts. Earn rewards as you roll!

### 3. Screen Check:

Too much screen can fry the brain. Use the phone's Screen Time feature. Maybe swap that extra TikTok hour with something wild, like... I dunno, actual dancing?

Remember, time management isn't just some adult-y thing. It's a hack to make life feel like the ultimate game – where you're the main character, and you're here to win! 🕹️🚀◎

## *Quick Challenge:*

Try both! Tonight, scribble tomorrow's tasks on paper. Then, pick an app and digitize them. Which felt better? No right answer, just find what's magic for you!

Your time's your currency. Spend it well, and you'll be living life in the fast lane, with zero speed bumps. Ready to roll? 🚗💨🎉

# Chapter 5: Hygiene & Grooming - Unlocking the Super-Clean, Super-Confident You!

## Hygiene and grooming? They're your power-ups

1. **Boost Your Confidence**: Good hygiene isn't just about cleaning dirt; it's about feeling like a champ. When you're groomed well, you walk taller and feel bolder.

2. **Ace First Impressions**: Ever judged a book by its cover? First impressions are vital. Whether it's for school, a date, or new friends, a neat appearance makes you instantly likable.

3. **Stay Healthy**: Good hygiene isn't just skin-deep. It's your shield against germs and illnesses. Keeping clean now means fewer problems in the future.

In short, proper grooming isn't just for looking good in selfies. It's about leveling up in life, feeling proud, and tackling any challenge with confidence.

## *All About That Base*

**1. Shower Power: It's Not Just About Smelling Good**:
  **Why Daily?**: Skin naturally produces oils and sheds dead cells. Daily showers help wash these away, preventing potential skin issues and keeping you fresh.

  **Temperature Talk**: Super hot showers? Tempting, but they can strip your skin of essential oils. Aim for warm showers and maybe a cool rinse at the end to seal those pores.

  **Lather, Rinse, Repeat**: Use a gentle body wash that suits your skin type. Remember, your body skin is different from your face; it can usually handle stronger washes.

**2. Choosing the Right Body Wash**:
  **Know Your Skin**: Dry skin? Look for moisturizing washes. Oily? Go for something balancing. Remember, the right body wash can make your post-shower skin feel amazing.

  **Natural vs. Chemical**: There's a big debate over natural ingredients versus chemical ones. It's about what works for YOU. Some people swear by organic products, while others find scientifically-developed ones more effective.

## 3. The Scent of You:

**Perfumes, Colognes, and Deodorants**: These are not just to mask bad odor but to accentuate your personal style. A signature scent can be memorable and make you stand out in a crowd.

**How to Choose?**: Test on your wrist, wait a few minutes, then smell. Scents can change upon reacting with your skin. And remember, sometimes less is more. A gentle hint of a scent can be more appealing than an overpowering aroma.

**Placement Points**: Apply to pulse points: wrists, behind the ears, and even behind the knees. The warmth helps diffuse and amplify the aroma.

**Rotate & Refresh**: Just like you wouldn't wear the same outfit every day, consider having a few scents to rotate. This way, you can match them with your mood or the occasion.

In a world of sensory overload, feeling clean, fresh, and smelling great can make a huge difference not just to others, but how you feel about yourself. Dive into this world with curiosity and find what resonates with you!

## *Daily Face Care – Smooth Moves*

**Staying Smooth**: Daily care is like feeding and leveling up your game avatar. Except, the avatar is your skin. You want it to perform at its best, right?

## 1. **Moisturizing Magic**:

**Why Moisturize?**: Ever notice how leather looks when it dries out? Well, skin can feel the same without hydration. Moisturizing helps maintain your skin's balance, keeping it soft and reducing the appearance of wrinkles. Think of it as a daily dose of water for your skin from the outside.

**Pick Your Potion**: Oily, dry, combination, sensitive...whatever your skin type, there's a moisturizer out there. Look for one tailored to your needs. For instance, oily skin? Go for a light, water-based product. Super dry? Cream-based is your friend.

**Routine Matters**: Clean your face. Apply in circular motions. Do it every day. Morning and night. Make it as habitual as brushing your teeth!

## 2. **Shield Against the Sun**:
**UV Rays: The Invisible Foe**: While the sun gives us warmth and Vitamin D, it also emits harmful UV rays. These can lead to sunburns, age spots, and even serious issues like skin cancer.

**Slay with Sunscreen**: Think of it as your daily armor. Even on cloudy days, UV rays can reach your skin. Whether it's a sunny beach day or a winter morning, don't skip this step.

**Beyond Lotions**: Sunscreens come in many forms: creams, gels, sticks, and sprays. Choose what feels right. And remember, if you're out for long or swimming, reapply!

Your face is what the world sees first. And like any main character in a game, it deserves the best gear and care. Stay smooth, stay shielded, and keep glowing!

## *Acne Attacks: Behind the Red Alert*

We've all had those mornings. You wake up, stroll to the mirror, and bam—a pimple announces its presence. But why? Here's a closer look:

**Hormonal Changes**: Especially common during teenage years, fluctuations in hormones can lead to increased oil production. That oil, or sebum, can clog pores leading to breakouts.

**Stress**: The body reacts to stress by producing more androgens, another type of hormone. This can stimulate hair follicles and oil glands, making acne more likely.

**Diet Choices**: Some research suggests that certain foods, especially dairy and high-glycemic-index foods (think white bread and chips), may be linked to breakouts.

**Combat Strategies: Know Your Arsenal**

**Cleansers**: These products contain salicylic acid or benzoyl peroxide, which can help unclog pores and reduce bacteria. A good cleanser can help you gently remove excess oil, which can be a lifesaver.

**Topical Treatments**: Products containing retinoids or antibiotics can target different aspects of acne. Retinoids speed up the skin's natural turnover process, and antibiotics fight bacteria.

**Moisturizers**: A non-comedogenic moisturizer (that means it won't clog your pores) is vital. Acne treatments can dry out your skin, and a moisturizer balances this out.

**Check the Label**: When choosing skincare products, understanding the ingredients is essential. Ingredients like hyaluronic acid hydrate, while niacinamide can reduce inflammation. Meanwhile, alpha and beta hydroxy acids can help exfoliate and clear dead skin cells.

The world of skincare might seem vast, but understanding the basics of what's in your products and how they work against acne can make all the difference. Remember, every skin type is unique, so it might take some experimenting to find what works best for you. If in doubt, consulting a dermatologist can provide tailored advice.

## Hair Today, Gone Tomorrow: Hair Care & Styles

**1. Shampoo Strategist**:
- **The Science Behind the Bubbles**: Shampoos contain surfactants that trap oils, dirt, and product residues. When you rinse, all these unwanted substances go down the drain, leaving your hair clean.
- **Picking the Right Product**: Not all shampoos are created equal. They're formulated for different hair types and concerns. Oily hair? A clarifying shampoo might be your best friend. Dry or curly? Hydrating or creamy

shampoos can be your hair's savior. Color-treated? Opt for sulfate-free options to maintain that hue.

- **Don't Overdo It**: Washing daily can strip your scalp of essential oils, leading to overproduction of oil or drying out. For many, every 2-3 days is a sweet spot, but listen to your hair's needs!

## 2. Conditioner Chronicles:

- **Silky Science**: Conditioners smooth down the hair cuticle (the outermost part of the hair shaft) that might get roughed up during washing. This leads to smoother, shinier hair.
- **Why It's a Game-Changer**: Apart from adding shine, conditioners prevent hair tangling, reduce breakage, and can even offer some protection from UV rays.
- **Application Technique**: Focus conditioner on the mid-length to ends of your hair, not the scalp. This way, you nourish the oldest and most damaged parts without weighing down your roots or making the scalp oily.

## 3. Trendy Trims:

- **Cutting for Health**: Regular trims prevent split ends from working their way up, which can lead to breakage and thin-looking ends. It keeps hair looking fresh and healthy.
- **How Often to Snip**: For shorter, defined styles, every 4-6 weeks might be necessary to maintain the shape. Longer hair might need a trim every 8-12 weeks. But remember, the exact timeline can depend on your hair's growth rate and style.
- **Stay in Style**: Regular trims also allow you to experiment with styles, stay updated with trends, or maintain a signature look that complements you best.

Hair is often called our "crowning glory," and with good reason. It can dramatically affect how we feel and how others perceive us. Dive into your hair care journey, armed with knowledge and an open mind!

## *Oral Odyssey: Dentals and Breath Boosts*

### 1. Tooth Tactics:

**Bristle Basics**: Did you know the average person spends 38 days brushing their teeth over a lifetime? Those tiny bristles on your toothbrush work hard, moving plaque and food particles away. For effective cleaning, choose a toothbrush with soft bristles and replace it every 3-4 months.

**Floss Like a Boss**: Flossing isn't just a dance move; it's the only way to remove food and plaque from between your teeth and under the gumline. Brushing alone misses about 40% of your tooth surfaces. So, if you're not flossing, you're not fully cleaning.

**Consistency is Key**: Brush at least twice a day, and don't forget to floss! Consistency ensures that plaque doesn't harden into tartar – a harder, stickier version that can lead to gum disease.

### 2. Breath Boss:

**Know the Culprits**: Foods like onions, garlic, and coffee can leave your breath less than fresh. But guess what? Most bad breath comes from bacteria in your mouth, especially the back of the tongue.

**Stay Hydrated**: A dry mouth is a haven for odor-causing bacteria. Drink water throughout the day, and you might just dodge dragon breath.

**Scrape and Rinse**: Consider using a tongue scraper to remove the thin layer of mucus and bacteria from your tongue. Following up with a mouthwash can offer added protection and freshness.

Your mouth is a gateway to the rest of your body, and good oral hygiene is about more than just a bright smile. It's a critical part of your overall health and well-being. So, flash those pearly whites and breathe easy, knowing you're on top of your oral game!

## *Hands & Feet Fleet: Nail Care*

### 1. Nailing It:
**Nails: The Nature's Claw**: Before forks and spoons, humans used nails as tools for digging and scratching. Now, we mostly use them to open soda cans or tap on our phones. But remember, hygiene first!

**Cuticle Chronicles**: Fun fact: Cuticles are like the bouncers of a club – they protect your nails from bacterial party crashers. So, give them respect. Push 'em gently, don't cut!

**File-O-Fun**: Ever played a violin? If yes, then you get it – one direction only. Same with nail filing! It helps to avoid the dreaded nail split orchestra.

## 2. Foot Forward:

**Smelly Feet Saga**: Our feet have more sweat glands than any other part of the body. So, when your sneakers start smelling like they've been to a cheese festival, it's time to air them out.

**Shoe-perstar Advice**: Your shoes are like houses for your feet. Would you want to live in a cramped, dark space? Nah. Give your feet some airy rooms!

## Grooming Gadgets: Essential Tools for Your Kit

### 1. Tool Time:

**Razors**: They've come a long way from shark teeth and flint blades (yes, ancient people were hardcore!). Modern razors are your sleek ally against rogue hairs.

**Tweezers**: The Swiss Army Knife of grooming. Perfect for eyebrow battles and those annoying splinters that think your fingers are a nice place to vacation.

**Nail Clippers**: Back in the day, folks used to sharpen their nails on rough surfaces. Today? We've got these cool clippers. Separate ones for hands and feet, because of hygiene.

**Brushes & Combs**: Imagine grooming a lion's mane. Exciting? Nope. But with the right comb or brush, your wild hair can be tamed into submission.

Embrace the grooming journey! Because every time you take care of yourself, you're like a car getting an upgrade. Zoom zoom!

# The Scent Scene: Understanding Deodorants & Perfumes

### 1. Smell Well:

**History Whiff**: Did you know that the first deodorants were used by ancient Egyptians? They used to apply spices and citrus oils to smell good in the scorching heat. Talk about staying fresh in the desert!

**Deodorant vs. Perfume**: Think of it this way: Deodorants are like your personal defense against the dark arts of body odor. Perfumes? They're like your charm spell. Use them wisely, and you're magic!

**Spritz Science**: Perfumes have top, middle, and base notes. It's like a music symphony for your nose! The first scent you get? That's the top note. Wait a while, and you'll get to the heart of the perfume.

**Rule of Thumb (or Wrist)**: When testing scents, spray on your wrist, wait a moment, and then take a whiff. It lets the perfume mix with your natural scent, creating a unique combo just for you.

## Challenge Time! 7-Day Grooming and Self-Care Challenge

### Day 1: Hair Dare

Try a new hairdo. Maybe a slicked-back look? Or just let it flow free. Use a hair product you haven't before, like a gel or a new shampoo.

**Day 2: Scent-ventures**

Test a new deodorant or cologne. Pick something that matches your mood for the day. Fresh? Spicy? Woodsy? How does it make you feel?

**Day 3: Face First**

Dive into face care. Try a gentle face wash or a scrub. How's that face feeling post-cleansing? Fresh as morning dew?

**Day 4: Footloose Fun**

Give those feet some attention. Scrub away, moisturize, and wear your comfiest or coolest socks. Notice the difference as you strut your stuff.

**Day 5: Nail It**

Spend some time on nail care. Clean, clip, and maybe even buff. How do those hands look post-manicure? Pro-level, right?

**Day 6: Style Swipe**

Mix up your style. Wear something you wouldn't usually wear, or pair things differently. Maybe those sneakers with that shirt? Fashion-forward or laid back, it's your call.

**Day 7: Reflect and Respect**

Spend some time in front of the mirror. Look at the changes from the past week. Feel the confidence, notice the details, and pat yourself on the back. You did it!

At the end of the week, jot down your thoughts. Which day was your favorite? Did you discover a new style or grooming habit you loved? How did these small changes make you feel?

# Chapter 6: Talkin' the Talk – Chatting with Parents (and Later, Teachers and Bosses)

## Why Chat Matters

Before we jump in, let's get why this is crucial. It's not just about avoiding lectures or earfuls, it's about building relationships. Yes, even with your boss or that math teacher who loves trigonometry too much.

## Active Listening – The Super Skill

You know that feeling when you're telling a story, and your friend is just staring at their phone? Annoying, right? Now imagine how your parents feel. Active listening isn't just nodding and saying "uh-huh". It's about:

**Being All There**: Put away distractions. Yes, that means your phone.
**Eye Contact**: This doesn't mean a staring contest, but occasional eye contact tells them you're engaged.
**Open Body Language**: Unfold those arms and lean in a bit. It screams, "I'm listening!"

Fun Fact: Most folks just want to feel heard. Once they do, they're way more chill.

## Repeat & Clarify:

So, your mom just gave you a 10-minute lecture about cleaning your room. Instead of rolling your eyes, try this:

**Mirror Back**: "So, you'd like me to clean my room every Sunday, right?"
**Ask Questions**: "Would it be okay if I did it in the evening instead of the morning?"

This does two cool things:

1. Shows you were paying attention (Brownie points!).
2. Clears up any confusion before it becomes a bigger deal.

### *Mutual Satisfaction – The Win-Win Situation*

Think about what they're asking from your point of view.
Think about it from their point of view. (Trust us, it helps.)

Now, find a middle ground. It's like trading Pokémon cards. You give a little, you get a little.

## It's All in the Delivery:

How you say it can be as important as what you're saying. Keep it calm, throw in a smile, and be open to compromise. Remember: It's not about winning. It's about understanding and being understood.

## Homework (Don't Groan!):

Next time you chat with your folks or anyone "in charge," use these tricks. Jot down how it went. Did it feel different? How did they react? Reflect and level up those convo skills!

## Mastering the Art of Gentle Decline & Convincing Convo

### 1. The Gentle No:

Every "no" isn't created equal. Sometimes a straight "no" is like a red rag to a bull. Let's soften the impact:

**"Not Now"**: "Can I finish my homework first?"
**Offer Alternatives**: "How about we do it this way instead?"
**Gratitude First**: "I appreciate you thinking of me, but…"

Pro Tip: Avoidance rarely works. It's like trying to dodge rain – eventually, you'll get wet!

## 2. Speak Up, But Wisely:

Want to voice disagreement without setting off fireworks? Here's how:

**Stay Calm & Collected**: Shouting matches? Nope. Always stay level-headed.
**Use "I" Statements**: "I feel overwhelmed when…" It's less accusatory.
**Ask Questions**: "Have you ever felt like this?"

## 3. Emotional Arguments – Handle with Care:

Emotions are like spices in cooking: a little goes a long way.

**Express Your Feelings**: It's okay to let them know how you feel, but...
**Avoid Emotional Overload**: An emotional volcano is impressive, but not productive.

Funny Fact: Ever noticed how, in movies, characters bond during emotional moments? Real life isn't too different. Emotions can bridge gaps – if used right.

## 4. Validation Junction:

This is the place where you acknowledge their feelings, even if you don't agree. It's like saying, "I see where you're coming from."

**Empathize**: "I understand why you might feel that way…"
**Reiterate**: "So, you're saying..." It shows you're listening.

## *Real-life Challenge*

Next disagreement or discussion you have, put these tactics to the test. Notice any change in the vibe of the conversation? Bonus points if you can turn a potential argument into a chill chat!

# Chapter 7: Find Your Fit: The Power-Up Exercise Guide

## Muscle Science 101

Muscles are kinda like plants. 🌱 You water a plant, give it sunlight, and it grows, right? Similarly, when you exercise, you're "feeding" your muscles. And like a plant getting bigger and greener, muscles get stronger and more toned.

Funny Fact: Muscles don't grow *during* your workout. They actually grow *after*. It's like they're saying, "Whoa, that was hard, let's prep for next time!"

## The Daily Dose:

Every day a little bit makes a big difference.

**Consistency is Key**: Imagine if you watered the plant only once a month. Not good, right? Muscles thrive on regular "feeding."
**Mix it Up**: Don't do the same thing every day. Muscles get bored too! Rotate between squats, push-ups, and planks.
**Rest Up**: Muscles need their beauty sleep. One or two days of rest in a week is when the real magic happens.

## Feel Good, Look Good:

Exercise isn't just about looking swole. It's like a happiness injection:

**Mood Boost**: Exercise releases happy chemicals called endorphins. Feeling down? A quick workout can be a mood-lifter!
**Energize**: It sounds backward, but moving actually gives you more energy.
**Confidence**: Knowing you're doing something good for yourself? Best. Feeling. Ever.

Pro Tip: Not a fan of hardcore workouts? Dance, walk, or even just stretching counts. The point is to move!

# Understanding the Main Muscle Groups

**Upper Body**:

**Chest**: The powerhouse for push movements like push-ups.
**Back**: Essential for pull movements and posture. Think of activities like rowing.
**Shoulders**: Provide width to the upper body and are used in lifting and rotation actions.
**Biceps and Triceps**: Front and back of the upper arm, used for lifting and pushing.

**Core**:

**Abdominals**: Front muscles that give the sought-after "six-pack" look.
**Obliques**: Side muscles aiding in rotation and side bending.
**Lower back**: Stabilizes the spine and supports posture.

**Lower Body**:

**Quadriceps**: Front thigh muscles, active in squatting and lunging.
**Hamstrings**: Back thigh muscles, essential for bending the knee and hip extension.
**Calves**: The muscles in the back of the lower leg, used in walking, running, and jumping.
**Glutes**: Your buttock muscles, key players in walking, running, and standing up.

Remember, every individual's body is unique, and while understanding the basics is essential, tuning in to one's body's specific needs is crucial.

# Rocking Out with Key Exercises for Each Muscle Group 🎸

## Upper Body:

**Push-ups**: A full-body workout that focuses on the chest, shoulders, and triceps. Remember to keep your body in a straight line, from head to heels.

**Dumbbell Rows**: Great for strengthening the back muscles. Stand with a dumbbell in each hand, bend over slightly, and pull the weights towards your hip.

**Shoulder Presses**: Using dumbbells, this exercise targets the shoulders. Start with the weights at shoulder height and press upwards until your arms are fully extended.

**Bicep Curls**: Hold a dumbbell in each hand and, keeping your elbows close to your body, lift the weights towards your shoulders.

**Tricep Dips**: Using a bench or a stable surface, position your hands shoulder-width apart, move your body forward, and bend your elbows to lower your body.

## Core:

**Planks**: A fantastic exercise for the entire core. Keep your body straight, elbows under your shoulders, and hold.

**Bicycle Crunches**: Lying on your back, bring your right elbow and left knee towards each other while straightening the other leg. Switch sides for a pedaling motion.

**Russian Twists**: Sit on the floor, lean back slightly, and rotate your torso to tap the floor beside you, switching sides.

**Back Extensions**: Lie face down, arms at your sides, and lift your upper body off the ground, using your lower back muscles.

## Lower Body:

**Squats**: Stand with feet shoulder-width apart, and lower your body as if you're sitting in a chair. Great for the quads, hamstrings, and glutes.

**Lunges**: Step forward and bend both knees at a 90-degree angle, keeping your front knee above your ankle.

**Calf Raises**: Standing upright, push through the balls of your feet to raise your body upward.

**Glute Bridges**: Lie on your back, knees bent, and lift your hips off the ground by squeezing your glutes.

Beginners should consider starting with a comfortable number of repetitions and gradually increase as strength and endurance build. Always consult with fitness professionals or PE teachers to ensure correct techniques.

# Here's What NOT to Do in Fitness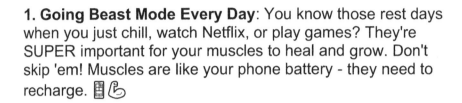

**1. Going Beast Mode Every Day**: You know those rest days when you just chill, watch Netflix, or play games? They're SUPER important for your muscles to heal and grow. Don't skip 'em! Muscles are like your phone battery - they need to recharge. 🔋💪

**2. Lifting Super Heavy... Without the Know-How**: Wanting to flex with heavy weights? Cool! Just make sure you've nailed the form first. Picture this: You wouldn't try to race a car if you didn't know how to drive, right? Same deal. Avoid injuries and get guidance if you're unsure.

**3. The "Why Can't I Do That?" Syndrome**: See someone lifting more, running faster, or just being all-around more ripped? It's cool to admire, but don't beat yourself up over it. Your fitness journey is like your favorite playlist – unique to you! 🎧

**4. The Supplement Superstore**: Heard of those magical powders and pills promising mega muscles and instant energy? Slow down! While some might help, remember this: those colorful fruits, veggies, and good ol' proteins from whole foods? They're your real MVPs when it comes to nutrients.

# One-Week Fitness Jam! 💢

## 🎸 Monday - Rock those Arms & Beat the Streets!
**Upper Body**: Start with a fun circuit of push-ups, dumbbell rows, and bicep curls. Aim for 3 sets of 10-12.
**Cardio**: Lace up those shoes and hit the streets for a 20-minute jog. Play your favorite tracks to keep you moving!

## 🏋 Tuesday - Leg Day Grooves & Stretchy Moves
**Lower Body**: Dive into squats, lunges, and calf raises. Aim for 3 sets of 12.
**Flexibility**: Unwind with a 15-minute stretch session. Focus on your hamstrings, quads, and calves.

## 🍕 Wednesday - Chill Mode Day
Relax with some light activity. Maybe take a casual stroll around the neighborhood, pet some dogs, grab a smoothie.

## 🔥 Thursday - Core Party & Skip to the Beat
**Core**: Crush it with planks, bicycle crunches, and Russian twists. 3 sets each, and feel the burn!
**Cardio**: Grab a jump rope and channel your inner boxer. Skip away for 15 minutes, and see if you can do some tricks!

## 🌈 Friday - Balance it Out with Upper Vibes
**Upper Body**: Cycle back to shoulder presses, tricep dips, and another round of push-ups. 3 sets of 10-12.
**Balance**: Challenge yourself! Try single-leg stands and other fun balance exercises for 10 minutes. Pretend you're surfing or doing yoga on a mountain!

### 🎠 Saturday - Weekend Warrior Mode

Dive into whatever makes you move! Shoot some hoops, cycle with friends, or dance in your room. Just have a blast and keep active.

### 🍶 Sunday - The Ultimate Rest & Chill

Grab your favorite snacks, binge a show, or read that book you've been eyeing. Your body needs it, and hey, you've earned it!

Remember, the key is consistency and having fun! Adjust as needed, and soon enough, you'll be rocking that fit life! 🎶🤘

**Takeaway Challenge**: Snap a before pic. Trust me, after a month, you'll be amazed at the progress. And, pics or it didn't happen, right? 😊

# Chapter 8: Foodie Fundamentals - Unleashing Your Inner Chef

## Why Cook? The Sizzling Benefits

Ever heard, "You are what you eat"? It's kinda true! Here's why you should trade that instant noodle packet for a chef hat:

**Health Hero**: Know what's in your food. No hidden nasties!
**Money Saver**: Cooking at home? Way cheaper than eating out or ordering in.
**Impress & Express**: Friends dig it when you whip up a mean sandwich. Plus, cooking is an art! 🎨
**Adulting 101**: Master this, and you're one step closer to that grown-up badge.

**Brain Boost**: Fun fact: Cooking uses math, reading, timing...
It's a brain workout!

*Pyramid Power: The Food Pyramid Basics*

It's like building blocks, but for food!

**Base Layer**: Grains. Think bread, rice, pasta. It's your body's fav energy source.

**Next Up**: Fruits and Veggies. Nature's candy and packed with vitamins.

**Middle Tier**: Protein. From meat to tofu, it's all about muscle-building.

**Just a Hint**: Dairy. Great for bones but take in moderation.

**Tiny Top**: Fats, oils, and sweets. Treat yourself, but not too often!

Pro Tip: Imagine your plate as this pyramid. More grains and veggies, less of the sugary stuff.

# Vitamins Unveiled: What, Why, and Where?

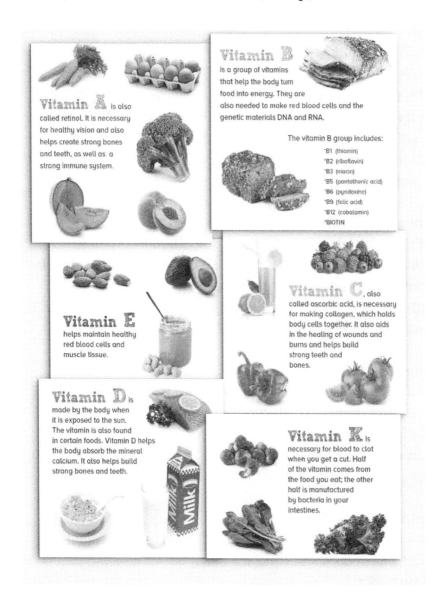

**Vitamin A** is also called retinol. It is necessary for healthy vision and also helps create strong bones and teeth, as well as a strong immune system.

**Vitamin B** is a group of vitamins that help the body turn food into energy. They are also needed to make red blood cells and the genetic materials DNA and RNA.

The vitamin B group includes:

- B1 (thiamin)
- B2 (riboflavin)
- B3 (niacin)
- B5 (pantothenic acid)
- B6 (pyridoxine)
- B9 (folic acid)
- B12 (cobalamin)
- BIOTIN

**Vitamin E** helps maintain healthy red blood cells and muscle tissue.

**Vitamin C**, also called ascorbic acid, is necessary for making collagen, which holds body cells together. It also aids in the healing of wounds and burns and helps build strong teeth and bones.

**Vitamin D** is made by the body when it is exposed to the sun. The vitamin is also found in certain foods. Vitamin D helps the body absorb the mineral calcium. It also helps build strong bones and teeth.

**Vitamin K** is necessary for blood to clot when you get a cut. Half of the vitamin comes from the food you eat; the other half is manufactured by bacteria in your intestines.

## Vitamin A (Retinol)

**What's the big deal?** This vitamin is like a guardian for your eyes, helping you see in dim light. Plus, it keeps your skin smooth and boosts the immune system.

**Munch on**: Carrots, sweet potatoes, spinach, kale, and fish. The carrot thing isn't just a myth; they genuinely can help your vision!

### Vitamin B (Complex)
**What's the big deal?** It's not just one vitamin, but a group that plays a critical role in converting food into energy. They also help maintain healthy skin, eyes, and nerve functions.
**Munch on**: Whole grains, beans, peas, and nuts. Avocado toast, anyone?

### Vitamin C (Ascorbic acid)
**What's the big deal?** A real superstar when it comes to boosting your immune system. It also helps wounds heal faster and enhances iron absorption.
**Munch on**: Oranges, strawberries, bell peppers, and broccoli. Perfect for when flu season strikes!

### Vitamin D
**What's the big deal?** Without it, your bones would feel like jelly because it aids in calcium absorption. Plus, it plays a role in mood regulation and immune system support.
**Munch on & Soak in**: Fish, fortified dairy products, and sunlight. That's right, chilling in the sun can give you a dose!

### Vitamin E (Tocopherol)
**What's the big deal?** This vitamin is like a shield, protecting your cells from damage. Plus, it's essential for immune function and skin health.
**Munch on**: Nuts, seeds, spinach, and broccoli. Basically, it's nature's skincare!

**Vitamin K**

**What's the big deal?** This one's crucial for blood clotting, so if you get a cut, it won't keep bleeding.

**Munch on**: Green leafy veggies, fish, and meat.

**The Secret?** Eating a balanced diet with a mix of these vitamin-rich foods can help keep your body and mind in tip-top shape. So, next time you're munching on a carrot, just know you're boosting your superhuman powers.

**Quick Bites: Fast, Tasty, Nutritious**:

Let's face it; we all love quick and easy. Here are some slam dunk recipes:

**Morning Kickstart**: Overnight oats. Just toss in yogurt, oats, and fruits. Morning = sorted.

**Lunch Box Hero**: Chicken or tofu salad wrap. Veggies, a bit of dressing, and you're set.

**Dinner Quickie**: Stir-fry! Veggies, protein, some sauce. Sizzle, sizzle!

# *Cooking 101: The Processes that Make Magic*

## 1. Boiling:

**Step-by-Step:**
1. Choose a pot that fits your food plus enough water to cover it.
2. Fill the pot with water, leaving some space at the top to prevent spills.
3. Turn the stove on high and wait for the water to start bubbling.
4. Once boiling, add a pinch of salt.
5. Add your chosen food (like pasta or veggies).
6. Reduce the heat if it starts bubbling too violently.
7. Once cooked (pasta becomes soft, veggies become tender), drain the water using a strainer.

## 2. Grilling:

**Step-by-Step:**
1. Clean the grill grates to avoid old residue.
2. Preheat the grill on medium-high heat.
3. Lightly oil the grates (a towel dipped in oil works great).
4. Place your food on the grill.
5. Keep an eye out for grill marks, then flip the food.
6. Once both sides have marks and the inside is cooked, remove from the grill.

## 3. Baking:

**Step-by-Step:**
1. Start by preheating your oven to the required temperature.

2. Prepare your food or mix (like cookie dough or cake batter).

3. Place in an oven-safe dish or on a baking sheet.

4. Slide it into the oven.

5. Set a timer for the recommended duration.

6. Once done, test with a toothpick (it should come out clean for cakes).

7. Remove from the oven and let cool.

## 4. Sautéing:

**Step-by-Step:**

1. Pick a frying pan or skillet.

2. Heat a small amount of oil or butter over medium-high heat.

3. Add thinly sliced or diced food to the pan.

4. Stir or toss regularly to ensure even cooking.

5. Cook until the food is browned or tender, then transfer to a plate.

## 5. Roasting:

**Step-by-Step:**

1. Preheat your oven.

2. Prep your food. This could be chopping veggies or seasoning meat.

3. Place on a roasting tray. You can use a rack for even heat distribution.

4. Slide the tray into the oven.

5. Cook for the recommended time, occasionally checking for desired tenderness or browning.

6. Once done, remove from the oven and allow to rest before serving.

# Decoding Recipes: Your Guide to Culinary Success

**Recipe Anatomy:** Before diving into the how-to, it's essential to understand the anatomy of a recipe. At its core, a recipe is a set of instructions. But to ensure that what you cook tastes as intended, you need to pay attention to these sections:

**Title:** Gives you an idea of the dish you're about to prepare.
**Preparation & Cooking Time:** Know how much time you need.
**Ingredients:** Lists everything you need. Always check you have them all before starting!
**Measurements:** The precise amounts of each ingredient. This can be in cups, tablespoons, grams, etc.
**Instructions:** The step-by-step guide to creating the dish.
**Serving Size:** Tells you how many people the dish will feed.
**Notes or Tips:** Some recipes include extra hints or variations.

**Reading and Using a Recipe Step-by-Step:**

1. **Skim Through:** Before doing anything, read the recipe from start to finish. This gives you a clear picture of the process, ensuring there are no surprises halfway through.

2. **Gather Your Ingredients:** Before you start, have all your ingredients measured out and ready. This is called "mise en place" in the cooking world, which is French for "everything in its place." It ensures a smooth cooking process.

3. **Follow the Order:** Most recipes list ingredients in the order you'll need them. The same goes for the instructions. Stick to the order unless you're an experienced cook and know a particular tweak.

4. **Keep an Eye on Cooking Terms:** Understand the basics, like 'dice,' 'chop,' 'simmer,' 'boil,' etc. If you're unfamiliar with a term, a quick online search can usually clarify it.

5. **Don't Rush:** Especially if it's your first time with a new recipe. Taking your time can be the difference between a successful dish and a culinary disaster.

6. **Taste as You Go:** Just because you're following a recipe doesn't mean you can't adjust. If you think it needs more salt, seasoning, or an ingredient, trust your palate.

7. **Make Notes:** If you feel something should be adjusted the next time, or if you made a tweak that worked, jot it down for future reference.

| 1 GALLON | 1 QUART | 1 PINT | 1 CUP | 1 OUNCE | 1 TBLSP | 1 TSP |
|---|---|---|---|---|---|---|
| 4 QUARTS | 2 PINTS | 2 CUPS | 16 TBSP | 2 TBSP | 3 TSP | 5 ML |
| 8 PINTS | 4 CUPS | 16 OUNCES | 8 OUNCES | 30 ML | 1/2 OUNCE | |
| 16 CUPS | 32 OUNCES | 480 ML | 240 ML | | 15 ML | |
| 128 OUNCES | 950 ML | | | | | |
| 3.8 LITERS | | | | | | |

Remember, while recipes provide structure, cooking is as much an art as it is a science. The more you practice, the better you'll become at adapting and making dishes on your own!

# Knives: The Right Blade for the Right Job

### UTILITY KNIFE
Mid-sized knives used for miscellaneous cutting
Larger than a paring knife but not as large as a chef's knife

### STEAK KNIFE
Used to slice steaks from whole cuts of meats such as sirloin and rump.

### CARVING KNIFE
Long , thin narrow blade with a sharply pointed tip which can slice and separate meat from bone

### CARVING FORK
Holds the material being cut in the correct position
Used in conjunction with a craving knife

### CLEAVER
Thick, wide and heavy blade – designed to force their way through meat or poultry bones. Width makes it ideal for pulverising meat, or crushing seeds or garlic

### PARING KNIFE
Used for intricate work and allow for greater amount of control than a larger knife

### BONING KNIFE
For removing bones and skinning meat or poultry

### CHEFS KNIFE
Most used kitchen knife – can be used for everything from chopping to slicing fruits and vegetables. Broad blade that curves upwards toward the tip to allow the knife to rock for fine mincing

### SANTOKU KNIFE
Japanese version of a chef's knife. Perfectly balanced
Traditionally shorter than chef and has less of a rocker

### BREAD KNIFE
Thick-bladed knife used for cutting loaves of bread. Have thick and deep serrated edges to cut through hard and thick crust.

**Knife Basics:** Did you know chefs often say that their most valuable tool isn't the stove or oven, but the knife? It's because a good, sharp knife can make your cooking prep faster, safer, and more efficient. But not all knives are created equal. Let's chop down the basics!

**Chef's Knife:** The MVP of the kitchen. It's usually 6-12 inches long and can handle a variety of tasks, from chopping vegetables to slicing meat. If you're buying just one knife, this should be it.

**Paring Knife:** Think of this as the chef's knife's little sibling. It's best for small tasks like peeling and trimming.

**Bread Knife:** Got serrations that look like little teeth. Perfect for—you guessed it—slicing bread!

**Utility Knife:** It's the in-between of a chef's and paring knife. Great for cutting fruits and veggies.

**Boning Knife:** Thin and flexible, this knife is for removing bones from meat. Not a must-have for beginners, but good if you're feeling adventurous.

**Serrated Utility Knife:** Similar to a bread knife but shorter. Good for tomatoes and other soft fruits.

**Safety First:** Always remember to:
Keep your knives sharp. Ironically, a sharper knife is safer because it requires less force and is less likely to slip.
Never catch a falling knife. Let it drop.
Hold the knife with a firm grip and use a 'claw grip' for the hand holding the food.

### Challenge Time

Grab a cookbook or find a YouTube channel. Try one new recipe a week. Snap a pic of your dish when done. Before you know it, you'll be the next teen chef sensation! 🔍❄

# Chapter 9: The Ultimate Guide to Stress-Free Laundry

**1. Sorting for Success:** Get your clothes sorted. Whites with whites, darks with darks, and delicates solo. Avoid the horror of a red sock turning everything pink!

**2. Check the Tags:** Those tiny tags inside your clothes? They've got super important washing instructions. No joke.

**3. Detergent Drama:** You've got a few options here!
   **Liquid Detergent:** Great for most washes. Good at treating stains if you apply a bit directly.
   **Powdered Detergent:** Typically cheaper and can be more eco-friendly.
   **Pods:** Convenient. Just throw one in, but make sure you're using the right amount for your load size.
   **Fabric Softener:** Makes clothes feel soft, smell fresh. But don't overdo it!
   **Bleach:** Only for whites when they get really dingy. And always handle with care!

**4. The Machine's Modes:**
   **Regular/Normal:** Your go-to for everyday stuff.
   **Delicate:** For the stuff that needs a soft touch.
   **Permanent Press:** Best for synthetic fabrics.

**5. To Dry or Not to Dry:** Remember, the dryer can shrink clothes! Some stuff might be better off air-drying.

**6. Folding & Storing:** Your clothes took a spa day; now give them a comfy home.

**Tips & Tricks:**

**Stains:** Act FAST. Treat them immediately.

**Zippers & Buttons:** Zip 'em up and unbutton to avoid snagging.

**Inside Out:** Especially for graphic tees to keep them sharp.

## *Decoding the Clothes Tags – Understanding Those Funky Symbols*

Ever noticed weird hieroglyphics on your clothes tags? They aren't ancient secrets; they're guidance on how to care for your attire! Let's decode!

**1.** The Basin: It's all about washing.

**Plain Basin:** Regular wash.

**Basin with Hand:** Hand wash only. No machines here!

**Basin with a '30' or '40':** This tells you the max temperature in Celsius to wash at.

**2. The Triangle:** Bleach guidance.

**Plain Triangle:** Bleach allowed.

**Triangled Crossed Out:** No bleach, mate. Ever.

**3. The Square:** Time to dry.

**Square with a Circle Inside:** You can tumble dry it.

**Square with Lines Inside:** Natural drying. Lines at the top mean to hang dry. Horizontal line in the middle? Lay flat to dry.

**4. The Iron:** Well, it's about ironing.

**Plain Iron:** Ironing's cool.

**Iron with Dots:** The number of dots indicates the recommended ironing temperature. One dot for low, two for medium, and three for hot.

**Iron with an 'X' Through It:** Never iron. Like, never.

**5. The Circle:** This one's about professional cleaning.

**Plain Circle:** Dry clean.

**Circle with an 'A' or 'P' Inside:** Specific chemicals the cleaner should use.

**Circle with an 'X' Through It:** Do not dry clean.

## *Quick Challenge!*

Grab three clothing items with different symbols. Can you decode their care instructions? Test your pals too! Who's the quickest tag reader?

# Chapter 10: Health, First Aid, and Meds: Staying Prepared and Safe!

## First Aid Basics

It's not about being a superhero; it's about knowing a few simple things that could make a huge difference.

### Cuts and Scrapes:
Clean the wound immediately with water and mild soap.
Apply a mild antiseptic if you have one.
Cover with a bandage to keep it clean.

### Burns:
Hold the burned area under cold running water for a few minutes.
Don't pop any blisters! They protect against infection.

Apply a burn ointment or aloe vera gel.

**Insect Bites and Stings:**
Remove the stinger with a card edge, if there's one.
Apply cold pack to reduce swelling.
Resist the itch! Scratching can lead to infection.

**When to Call for Help:** If someone's hurt bad or feeling super sick, it's essential to recognize when it's time to call the pros.

**Unconsciousness, severe bleeding, difficulty breathing:** Call for medical help immediately.

## *When Bleeding is Heavy: Immediate Responses to Control Bleeding*

1. **Tourniquet Application:**
   **What:** A tight band placed around an arm or leg to constrict blood flow.
   **Why:** Used to control life-threatening bleeding from a limb when direct pressure doesn't work. It stops blood flow to the injured area, preventing further loss.
   **Note:** Only use it as a last resort and note the time of application. Extended use can cause tissue damage.

2. **Elevation:**
   **What:** Lifting the injured area above the level of the heart.
   **Why:** Uses gravity to reduce blood flow to the injured area, limiting swelling and bleeding.

3. **Direct Pressure:**
   **What:** Firmly pressing a clean cloth or bandage onto the wound.

**Why:** Direct pressure on a wound helps the blood to clot, which reduces and eventually stops the bleeding.

### 4. Bending the Limb:
**What:** Using a roll or similar object and bending the limb at the injury.

**Why:** Bending can compress the blood vessels of the area, reducing blood flow and promoting clotting.

### 5. Vascular Compression:
**What:** Pressing on the blood vessel supplying the area, typically located above the injury.

**Why:** Temporarily stops the blood flow to the injured site, reducing blood loss.

### 6. Tamponade Technique:
**What:** Pressing a cloth or bandage deep into a wound.

**Why:** For deep or puncture wounds, this method applies pressure inside the wound to promote clotting and limit internal bleeding.

### 7. Pressure Bandage:
**What:** A bandage applied with enough pressure to prevent bleeding but not so tight as to cut off circulation.

**Why:** Helps maintain continuous pressure on the wound after the bleeding has been controlled, promoting sustained clotting.

Always remember, these measures are first aid responses meant to stabilize the situation until professional medical assistance is available. If someone is injured, always seek medical attention promptly.

# Pill Talk: Navigating Common Over-the-Counter Medications

## Paracetamol (Acetaminophen)

### 1. What It Does:
Primarily an analgesic (pain reliever) and antipyretic (fever reducer).

### 2. Why It's Used:
To treat mild to moderate pain, such as headaches, menstrual cramps, or toothaches.
To reduce fever.

### 3. Safety and Precautions:
Always follow the recommended dosage. Overdose can be harmful and may lead to serious liver damage.
It's usually gentle on the stomach and doesn't cause stomach problems like some other pain relievers can.
Avoid consuming alcohol when taking Paracetamol.
Consult with a doctor if you have liver or kidney problems before taking it.

## Ibuprofen

### 1. What It Does:
It's an NSAID (non-steroidal anti-inflammatory drug) that provides analgesic (pain-relieving), antipyretic (fever-reducing), and anti-inflammatory effects.

### 2. Why It's Used:
To treat pain, inflammation, and fever. Useful for conditions like arthritis or after minor injuries.
To alleviate menstrual cramps.

### 3. **Safety and Precautions:**

Just like any NSAID, Ibuprofen can be harsh on the stomach and long-term usage or overdose can lead to gastrointestinal issues, like ulcers.

Always follow the recommended dosage. Taking more than the recommended amount can increase the risk of heart problems or strokes.

Do not consume alcohol when taking Ibuprofen.

Consult with a doctor if you have heart problems, high blood pressure, or kidney problems before taking it.

### General Guidelines:

Always read and follow the directions on the medicine label.
Store medicines out of the reach of children.
If in doubt about any medicine, consult with a pharmacist or doctor.
Never share your prescription or over-the-counter drugs with others.

Remember, while these medications are available without a prescription, it's essential to use them responsibly and be aware of potential interactions with other drugs or conditions. If unsure, always seek guidance from healthcare professionals.

### Antibiotics Explained: Navigating Bacterial Invasions

Let's delve into the intricate realm of pathogens and the pharmaceutical arsenal we deploy against them.

1. **Viral Intruders**: Viruses are microscopic agents that tend to exhibit rapid onsets, usually manifesting within a concise incubation period of 1-5 days. When observing an elevation in

lymphocyte counts via a blood test, it's indicative of a viral invasion. Moreover, a transparent nasal discharge or a clear runny nose is a hallmark of viral activity. And here's the pivotal point: antibiotics hold no efficacy against these viral entities.

2. **The Bacterial Brigade**: Contrarily, bacterial infections usually manifest with more pronounced symptoms, often accompanied by purulent discharges—like a greenish or yellowish hue in your cough or nasal mucus. This pus formation is a direct aftermath of bacterial activity. Furthermore, an escalated leukocyte count in a blood test points towards bacterial interference. Unlike their viral counterparts, bacterial infections are generally more insidious, unfolding and intensifying over a longer duration.

3. **Antibiotics: The Bacterial Countermeasure**: Antibiotics are specialized compounds tailored to target and neutralize bacteria. When faced with a bacterial onslaught, they serve as our primary line of defense, helping mitigate and eventually eradicate the infection. However, their indiscriminate usage, especially against viral infections, is not just futile but also detrimental, leading to antibiotic resistance.

In summary, discerning between viral and bacterial symptoms can pave the way for more precise and effective treatments. Always be cautious and consultative when it comes to antibiotic usage; they are potent tools but must be reserved for genuine bacterial challenges.

**Antihistamines Unveiled**: At times, our body's immune response goes overboard, treating benign particles like pollen or certain foods as threats. This reaction prompts the release of histamines, causing allergic symptoms like sneezing, itching, or even more severe reactions. Antihistamines come into play here. They block or reduce the action of histamines, helping alleviate or prevent allergic reactions. Think of them as the body's moderators, keeping overreactions in check.

## Safety First with Medications

Medications, while beneficial, come with rules:
**Dosage is Key**: Taking more than prescribed can be harmful, and less might be ineffective.
**Mixing Meds**: Combining different medications without professional advice can lead to adverse reactions. Even seemingly harmless over-the-counter meds can interact unpredictably with other substances.
**Storage**: Keep medicines in cool, dry places unless instructed otherwise. This preserves their efficacy and prevents unintended ingestion, especially by children.

**When in Doubt, Google Out!**: While the internet is a treasure trove of information, it's essential to remember that not all sources are reliable. If you're confused about a particular medicine, it's a good idea to Google it for more details. However, here's the golden rule: always validate your findings with a healthcare professional. The internet can inform, but your doctor prescribes. In essence, medications are beneficial allies in maintaining our health, but they demand respect. Knowledge, caution, and the guidance of professionals ensure we get the best out of them without unintended complications.

## Quick Challenge!

Create a mini first-aid kit for your room or backpack. Include bandages, antiseptic wipes, and any other essentials you think would be helpful. Remember, it's always better to be prepared!

# Chapter 11: The Friendship Formulas

## Chatting Up Classmates: From "Hey!" to BFFs in No Time

### 1. Breaking the Ice: Hello, Stranger!

**Compliment Camouflage**: Kick things off with a kind word. "Hey, love those sneakers!" – Compliments are the ultimate icebreakers.

**Homework Heroes**: "Ugh, did you get number 5 on the math homework?" It's a classic, and hey, you might even get some help out of it!

**Menu Musings:** "If they served this in a 5-star restaurant, what do you think they'd call it?" Turning school lunch into gourmet food critiques, because why not?

### 2. Going from Chat to Chatter:

**Weekend Whispers**: "Doing anything fun this weekend?" It's light, it's breezy, and it gives them the chance to invite you or for you to invite them.

**Series & Show Swap**: "Ever watched *Stranger Things*? No? Oh, you're in for a ride!" Sharing show recommendations is the teen equivalent of bonding over coffee.

**Sporty Splices**: Whether you love sports or know zilch about them, ask them about their favorites. You might learn something new, or at the very least, have someone to attend school games with.

### 3. Keeping the Convo Cooking:

**Meme Magic**: Sending over a funny meme or GIF is the modern-day 'thinking of you' card. Plus, it's a great conversation starter.

**Study Session Setups**: "Want to revise together for the history test?" It's productive and gives you both downtime to chat during breaks.

**Lunch Link-ups**: "I brought extra cookies today, want some?" Sharing is caring and a fantastic way to get some chat time in.

Remember, all friendships start with a simple conversation. So, pop that bubble of hesitation and start chatting! And most importantly, always be your quirky, wonderful self. It's way more fun that way!

# *Unmasking the Mystery of Making Mates*

1. **Common Ground Quest**: We all have something in common with others. Maybe it's a favorite band, a shared hobby, or just mutual disdain for early mornings. Find that link, and you've got a conversation starter.

2. **Consistency is Key**: Keep saying 'hello' and gradually build on those brief exchanges. Before you know it, you're talking about your weekend plans!

3. **Lend an Ear (or Two)**: Listen more than you speak. People appreciate a good listener. Remember, friendships are a two-way street.

4. **Activity Avenues**: Join clubs, groups, or sports that interest you. Shared activities create shared experiences, which can fast-track friendships.

5. **Open Invite Initiator**: Hosting a study group, movie night, or just a hangout? Opening up your space (even virtually) can be a great way to solidify a budding friendship.

6. **Ditch the Device**: When you're with potential new friends, put the phone away. Your TikTok feed can wait, but real-time bonding can't.

7. **Stay Genuine**: Pretending to be someone else is like wearing shoes that don't fit; it's uncomfortable and you won't get far. Be yourself; it's less work and a lot more fun.

8. **Respect Boundaries**: Everyone has them. If someone seems uninterested, don't take it personally. Move on, and find your tribe elsewhere.

9. **Laugh it Off**: Everyone messes up. Said something weird? Tripped in the hallway? Laugh about it. Showing you don't take yourself too seriously makes you approachable.

10. **Golden Rule Reminder**: Treat others how you'd like to be treated. It's classic, it's timeless, and it works. Plus, being kind is always in style.

**Challenge**: Try one of these techniques each day for the next week. By the end, see if you've made a new connection or strengthened an existing one. Good luck, friend-finder!

## Beware the Puppet Strings: Spotting Manipulation

Navigating friendships in the school years is like walking through a maze: it's fun, sometimes challenging, and there are occasional dead-ends. Among the many lessons, one essential is recognizing and dealing with manipulation. Think of it as learning to spot the 'shortcut cheaters' in the maze.

1. **Red Flags**: Manipulative people might often guilt-trip you, play the victim card, or give you silent treatments. It's like they have this secret remote, and they're trying to control your reactions. Stay alert!

2. **Flattery or Real Compliments?** They might butter you up with praises one minute, and the next, they're asking for a 'tiny' favor. It's the classic 'bait-and-switch'. Don't fall for it!

3. **Emotion Overload**: Manipulators are actors. They over-exaggerate their feelings to sway you. If every conversation feels like a roller-coaster of emotions, maybe it's time to reconsider that ride.

4. **Trust Your Gut**: Sometimes, something just feels off. It's like biting into a chocolate chip cookie and tasting raisins. Trust that feeling. It's your gut waving a little caution flag.

5. **The 'Always You' Game**: A manipulator will often shift blame. Dropped a pen? It's your fault. Alien invasion? Definitely your fault. Okay, maybe not that extreme, but you get the gist.

## *Mastering the Art of Dodging Puppet Strings: Avoiding Manipulation*

Alright, getting entangled in manipulation is like stepping into a puddle of super sticky, stubborn gum – no one plans for it, it's annoying, and you've got to get out of it without losing your shoe. Here's your handy guide to staying one step ahead of the puppet masters.

1. **Knowledge is Power**: Recognize the signs. As with any "boss level" in video games, knowing the manipulator's tactics is half the battle.

2. **"No" is a Complete Sentence**: Remember, you're not a doormat. It's okay to say no without a lengthy explanation. Own your decisions. If someone asks, "Why can't you do it?" A simple, "It doesn't work for me," is enough.

3. **Listen to Your Inner Detective**: If someone's story has more holes than your favorite cheese (or plot holes in a badly

72

written movie), question it. It's cool to be curious and ask for clarity.

4. **Avoid Over-Justifying**: You don't owe anyone a three-page essay on why you can't lend them your notes or join their plan. Keep it short and sweet.

5. **Delay Tactics**: If you're unsure, buy some time. "Let me think about it" or "I'll get back to you" can be your temporary shields.

6. **Physical Boundaries**: If someone is invading your personal space to gain an advantage (like that annoying 'over-the-shoulder' reader), take a step back. It's a clear sign without uttering a word.

7. **Stay Calm, Stay Cool**: Manipulators thrive on emotional reactions. Channel your inner Zen master. Breathe in, breathe out, and respond without getting heated.

8. **Seek Out Trustworthy Peers**: Just like in those epic adventure games, it's always good to have a trusty sidekick or two. Surround yourself with genuine people who've got your back.

9. **Regular Reality Checks**: Reflect on your interactions. Are they mostly give and not enough take? Balance is key in any relationship.

10. **Open Dialogue**: If you think a friend is unintentionally manipulative, address it. Sometimes, people don't realize their actions. A heart-to-heart can clear the air.

**Bonus Tip**: Create a 'Manipulation Jar'. Every time you spot and dodge a manipulation attempt, put a dollar (or any amount you want) in. At the end of the month, treat yourself. After all, dodging those puppet strings is worth celebrating!

Remember, life isn't about avoiding the storm, but learning to dance in the rain. With these tricks up your sleeve, you're ready to tango! 🕺💃

## *Exercise: Time to flex those observation muscles!*

1. **Diary Dive**: For the next week, at the end of each day, jot down moments in your interactions with friends that felt a bit 'off' or made you uncomfortable.

2. **Reflection Time**: At the end of the week, review your notes. Can you spot patterns or repeated behaviors that seem manipulative?

3. **Role Play**: With a trusted friend or family member, enact scenarios where you felt manipulated. Practice assertive responses. It's like rehearsing for a play, but the play is your life.

4. **Seek Guidance**: Share your feelings with a trusted adult or counselor. Sometimes, an external perspective can offer clarity.

Remember, genuine friends lift you up, celebrate your achievements, and stand by you. Everyone else? They're just lessons on your journey. Keep your head up!

# Chapter 12: Cybersecurity 101: Guarding Your Digital Fortress

## Cybersecurity 101

We live in a digital age. The days when your deepest secrets were written in a paper diary, secured with a small lock, are long gone. Now, it's about strong passwords and encrypted files. And just like the front door of your house, your digital accounts need to be securely locked to prevent unwanted guests from entering. If you wouldn't leave your front door wide open, why do the same with your personal accounts?

# The Need for Strong Passwords and Regular Updates

Think of a password as your digital shield. The stronger it is, the better protection you get. A password like "123456" or "password" is akin to using a wet paper bag as a shield (and we all know how that'll turn out!). Instead, mix it up! Combine upper and lower case letters, numbers, and special characters. For example, "Be@r$R0ck!" is much harder to crack than "bears".

Now, here's the trick: our digital world is evolving, and those pesky hackers are always leveling up. So, just as you outgrow clothes or get tired of last season's fashion, you need to change up your passwords. Updating them regularly ensures that even if someone does manage to guess one, they won't have it for long.

### Spooky Story: "The Haunting of the Hacked Account"

Jared loved video games. Every day after school, he'd dive into virtual realms, battling monsters, discovering treasures, and saving virtual worlds from destruction. He had an account where he'd saved all his progress, and it was his most prized possession.

One day, Jared received an email: "Password Reset Notification." Confused, he clicked on the email. He hadn't requested a password reset. As he opened his game, a sinking feeling hit him. All his progress, items, and scores had vanished. His account had been raided.

He later found out that his password, "Jared123", was easily guessed by a hacker who roamed these gaming platforms. The hacker not only stole his virtual treasures but began sending messages to Jared's friends, causing chaos and confusion. The haunting had begun.

Jared realized the importance of strong passwords too late. He had to start his gaming journey from scratch, but he made sure to equip himself with a more robust digital shield this time.

The lesson? Guard your virtual treasure just as fiercely as any pirate would! Ensure your passwords are strong and regularly updated, lest your digital world be haunted by the specters of the cyber realm.

## *Stranger Danger in the Digital Age*

**Be Cautious When Interacting Online**:
You know how we're always told, "Don't take candy from strangers"? Well, the digital world has its own version of this. Remember, it's easy for anyone to pretend to be someone else online. Whether it's on social media, gaming platforms, or chat forums, always be skeptical. Even if someone claims to be a fellow student or seems to know a lot about you, they might not be who they say they are. Keep your personal details private, don't share your location, and always let someone you trust know if a conversation feels off.

**Chilling Chronicle: "The Friendly 'Student' from Another School"**:

Jenny always loved making new friends. So when she received a friend request from Mike, who claimed to be a student from a nearby school, she didn't think twice before accepting. They chatted for weeks, talking about school, movies, and everything in between. Mike knew so much about the latest happenings in Jenny's school, it felt like he genuinely was from around the corner.

One day, Mike suggested they meet up at a local café. Jenny was hesitant but agreed. She told her best friend, Sarah, about it, who immediately felt something was amiss. They decided that Sarah would come along, but they'd sit separately. Jenny was to signal if she felt uncomfortable.

When Jenny got to the café, she was shocked. "Mike" was a man in his 40s, not a student like he'd claimed. As soon as she gave the signal, Sarah approached, pretending to be Jenny's older sister, and firmly told the man to leave.

Moral of the story? Always trust your gut, and never, ever meet up with an online acquaintance without taking precautions. You never know who's hiding behind that friendly profile picture.

## Beware the Bullies Beyond the Playground

**Strategies to Recognize and Avoid Online Bullying**:
Playgrounds aren't the only places bullies hang out. With screens becoming an essential part of our lives, some bullies have found a new haunt: the digital space. These cyberbullies can be stealthy, hiding behind anonymous usernames or even fake profiles. But no matter the mask, their intent is the same: to hurt and intimidate. It's essential to recognize signs of online

bullying: repeated negative comments, spreading rumors, or threats. If you're the target, don't engage. Document everything, block the user, and tell someone you trust. Remember, online bullies crave reactions. Don't give them the satisfaction.

**Sinister Tale: "The Echoing Insults of a Ghostly Chat Room"**:

Logan, an avid gamer, stumbled upon a chat room called "EchoRealm" one late evening. It promised discussions about the latest games, so he eagerly jumped in. Almost immediately, a user named "ShadowWhisperer" started making snide remarks about Logan's gaming choices.

Initially, Logan brushed it off, thinking ShadowWhisperer was just another troll. But soon, every time Logan commented, a barrage of insults followed. They weren't just about games anymore; they became personal, mocking his real-life appearance and interests.

Logan decided to leave EchoRealm, but the insults didn't stop there. ShadowWhisperer somehow found Logan's other social media profiles, flooding them with harsh comments and cruel memes.

Feeling trapped, Logan confided in his older sister, Lena. Using her tech skills, Lena traced the relentless bully's online presence back to... another student from Logan's school!

Confronted with evidence, the bully was taken aback, having never expected to be unmasked. The school intervened, and the cyberbullying came to an abrupt end. Logan learned the value of standing up against online intimidation, but more importantly, he realized the importance of seeking help when trapped in the echoing chambers of online malice.

## Too Much Information (TMI) Troubles

### The Perils of Oversharing Personal Information:
The Internet's vastness gives us the feeling of anonymity. But every picture, location tag, or personal tidbit we share creates a digital fingerprint. Sometimes, we think, "What's the harm in sharing just this one detail?" But piece by piece, we might unintentionally assemble a puzzle that reveals more about our lives than we'd like. Oversharing isn't just about TMI moments that make people cringe; it's about keeping personal information personal. Whether it's your current location, your daily routine, or even your pet's name (a common security question), think before you share.

### Mysterious Memoir: "The Snapchat Specter: When Every Share Haunts":
Emily was ecstatic about her solo trip to Paris. As a digital native, sharing her journey on Snapchat was second nature. From the croissant she had for breakfast to the unique street performer she met at Montmartre, her followers got real-time updates.

Midway through her trip, Emily started receiving snaps from an unknown user, "SpecterVue". The first snap was innocuous: just the Eiffel Tower sparkling at night. But then, they started to get more personal. A snap of the café she'd had breakfast in that very morning, followed by a picture of the very street performer she'd met.

Panic set in when she received a snap of her hotel, taken from a distance, with a caption: "Beautiful place you're staying at, isn't it?"

Emily immediately restricted her Snapchat settings and informed the local police. While the "Specter" was never caught, it served as a haunting reminder: every share can come back to haunt, so share with care.

## Safe Shopping in the E-Market

**Ensuring Your Purchases Are Secure and Trustworthy**: Online shopping is the modern-day magic carpet. With a few clicks, anything you desire can appear at your doorstep. But this convenience can come with caveats. Scams, fake products, and dodgy sellers lurk in the digital bazaars. Ensuring you shop from reputable sites, checking for secure payment gateways (look for that 'https' in the URL), and never saving your card details on sites that seem sketchy, are just a few ways to ensure your e-market experiences remain delightful, not dreadful.

**Creepy Chronicle: "The Online Order That Delivered... A Phantom?"**:
Ben was a gadget enthusiast. Late one night, while browsing an online forum, he stumbled upon an ad for a limited-edition smartwatch at a shockingly low price on a site called 'GizmoPhantom'. The deal was too enticing to resist.

A week after placing his order, he received a package. But inside wasn't the sleek smartwatch he had ordered. Instead, it was an old, tarnished pocket watch. Perplexed, Ben wound the watch, and it eerily started ticking backward.

That night, as Ben tried to sleep, he heard whispers. Looking around, he saw shadowy figures moving just beyond his peripheral vision. Each time he tried to focus on one, it would disappear. The only thing that seemed real in that room was the ticking of the strange pocket watch.

In a frenzy, Ben grabbed the watch, rushed to his backyard, and buried it. The whispers and shadows ceased instantly. The next day, 'GizmoPhantom' was nowhere to be found online. And all that remained of that terrifying night was a hole in the ground and a lesson about the dangers of too-good-to-be-true online deals.

## The Risks of Random Apps and Digital Dares

**Why It's Important to Vet Every Download**:
In the vast world of app stores, the colorful icons and promises of "the next big thing" can be tantalizing. From games that help you pass time to tools claiming to make life easier, the options seem endless. But here's the rub: not every app is designed with your best interests at heart. Some are thinly veiled traps, seeking permissions they don't need, only to access and misuse your personal data. So, before you hit that tempting 'download' button, do a quick background check. Read reviews, verify the developer, and question why a simple game needs access to your contacts or camera.

**Terrifying Tale: "The App That Asked for More Than Permissions"**:
Jenna was always keen to try the latest apps. One day, a friend mentioned 'MirrorMaze', a new augmented reality game. Without much thought, Jenna downloaded it. The game's

premise was simple: navigate through virtual mazes in your home using your phone's camera.

At first, it was fun, with virtual walls and challenges appearing in her living room. But things took a turn when the app prompted Jenna to enable nighttime mode. That night, she started the game, and it used her phone's flashlight to illuminate the dark rooms.

But instead of virtual walls, she saw eerie reflections of herself, each doing something different. One was crying, another laughing maniacally, and another just staring blankly back at her. The objective displayed on her screen read, "Find the REAL you."

Panicking, Jenna tried to close the app, but her phone was unresponsive. Every time she looked away and then back through the screen, the reflections got closer. Heart racing, she threw her phone onto her bed and watched as the screen slowly faded to black.
The next morning, she uninstalled 'MirrorMaze' and found that it had been removed from the app store. The reviews section was flooded with similar horrifying experiences from other users.

Jenna learned her lesson: always vet your downloads, because some apps want more from you than just a little storage space.

# Chapter 13: Emotions, relationship and love: From Fluttering Feelings to First Heartbreaks

## Emotions and Daydreams: Navigating the Heart's Labyrinths

**Understanding Your Feelings:**

***Welcome to the emotional roller coaster of your teenage years!*** Now, you might've heard adults say that, but here's the inside scoop: It's real, and everyone's ride looks a little different. Hormones, school stresses, the existential dread of what show to binge-watch next... a lot's going on. But these emotional twists and turns are also your body's cool (albeit confusing) way of growing up.

Have you ever felt an emotional cocktail of happiness, sadness, excitement, and confusion all in a day? Maybe even an hour? That's normal. Just remember: emotions are like weather patterns. They come, they go, and they don't define who you are. Instead, they give you a peek into how you perceive the world around you.

## Reality vs. Fantasy:

Okay, let's chat about those dreamy afternoons where you imagine becoming a YouTube sensation, starring in a blockbuster movie, or perhaps being crowned the next MasterChef. Daydreaming is a fabulous escape. It lets our brain take a little vacation and explore all the 'what-ifs.' But then reality checks in. And that's not bad!

Distinguishing between daydreams and reality is like knowing the difference between a movie and a documentary. Both are entertaining, but only one represents real events. It's okay to dream about being a superhero, but it's also essential to remember the real heroics in daily deeds, like helping a friend or acing that tricky math problem.

## Balancing Dreams with Reality:

Here's the exciting part: dreams can inspire reality! Think of them as the motivational posters of the mind. But for dreams to take flight, they need a solid runway to launch from - and that's where reality steps in.

Imagine if J.K. Rowling just daydreamed about Harry Potter but never wrote it down? Or if Elon Musk just fantasized about rockets but never built SpaceX? They anchored their dreams in the real world, and so can you!

Dream big, but also set realistic milestones. Want to be a singer? Start with singing lessons. Aim to be an environmentalist? Begin by reducing your carbon footprint. Every dream, when broken down, has small, achievable steps rooted in reality.

Remember, your emotions and dreams are like the wind beneath your wings. Sometimes turbulent, other times calm, but always guiding you through the adventure of growing up. Don't shy away from them, embrace them, and let them be your compass. After all, the sky's the limit!

## *Building a Relationship: Crafting a Connection That Lasts*

### Trust as the Foundation:

Imagine building a house. You wouldn't start with the roof, would you? Similarly, trust is the foundation of any healthy relationship. It's that solid ground upon which everything else is built. Without trust, relationships can crumble like a cookie in milk. Whether it's a friendship, romantic relationship, or just the camaraderie of a school project team, trust ensures that everyone's on the same page and that intentions are genuine.

When you trust someone, you believe in their words and actions. It's the confidence that they'll catch you during a trust fall exercise, both literally and metaphorically. Just remember, like any good foundation, trust needs time and care to solidify. So be patient, and let trust grow naturally.

**Open Communication and Mutual Respect:**

Ever played the game of 'Chinese whispers'? It's fun in a game setting but not in real life. Misunderstandings can lead to feeling like you're in a soap opera episode. The solution? Open communication. This means sharing your feelings, concerns, and joys. It's like giving someone the remote control to your personal thought-channel. But remember, it goes both ways. While you share, also be a good listener.

Now, onto mutual respect. Think of it as the golden rule: treat others the way you'd like to be treated. Respect is like the unsung hero in the background of every successful relationship story. It's recognizing the value in another person's thoughts, feelings, and experiences. Even if you don't always agree, you can still show respect by acknowledging their perspective.

**Setting and Respecting Boundaries:**

Boundaries in relationships are like invisible fences. They define what's okay and what's not. Whether it's about personal space, time, emotional needs, or online sharing limits, boundaries help keep the relationship respectful and comfortable for everyone.

Setting boundaries is like setting up your personal wifi network. You decide who gets access and to what extent. On the flip side, respecting someone else's boundaries is like not snooping around their personal files even if they give you the password. It's about mutual respect and understanding. And if you're ever in doubt about a boundary, just ask!

Building a relationship is like crafting a work of art. It requires patience, effort, and, most importantly, understanding each other's strengths and weaknesses. With these elements in place, you're well on your way to building connections that stand the test of time. After all, every masterpiece starts with a single brush stroke!

## *Seeing Beyond Illusions: The Real Deal in Relationships*

### Don't Overthink Every Little Thing:

Ever replayed a 10-second convo in your mind for 10 hours? Yep, we all have. Newsflash: Sometimes a "Hey" is just a "Hey". Not everything is a coded message. Overthinking can make simple chats seem like Sherlock mysteries. Chill, breathe, move on.

### If in Doubt, Just Ask:

Confused about that emoji or that vague text? Don't guess. Just ask. It clears up things faster than any guessing game and shows you're into the convo. Plus, be real when you chat. It's cool to be genuine. Trust us, people can tell.

### Stay True to Yourself:

Look, in a world of filters and FOMO, being genuine is gold. Embrace your quirks and be proud of them. When you're real with yourself, it's easier to be real with everyone else. Remember, the best version of you is the real you.

Life's too short for made-up dramas and deciphering coded messages. Keep it real, keep it clear, and watch how your relationships level up! 🚀 🎇

## The Art of Asking and Listening:

**Speak Up & Speak Out:**
You've got thoughts, questions, and cool opinions. Let them out! Unsure about something? Go ahead, ask away. Who knows? You might unlock a whole new level in a convo.

**Tune In, Drop Distractions:**
Listening isn't just about the ears; it's a full-sensory experience. So, the next time someone is sharing a story or their favorite meme, be all in. Your full attention could be the difference between a casual chat and a memory-making moment.

**Empathy: The Secret Ingredient:**
Want to know the recipe for deep connections? A dash of understanding, a sprinkle of patience, and a big dollop of empathy. Remember, being there doesn't mean having all the answers; sometimes, it's just about being present.

## Navigating the Pace and Boundaries of Love

**Love's Marathon, Not a Sprint:**
Rushing might be the norm in a world of instant noodles and quick texts, but love? It deserves the slow-cook treatment. Relish each moment and let the feels simmer.

**Draw That Line, But With Love:**
Setting boundaries isn't about building walls; it's about creating a safe space. Whether it's deciding how much time you spend together or being clear about your personal limits, it's all about mutual respect.

**It's a Dance, Not a Race:**
Relationships are a dance, with both partners leading at different times. Tune into each other's rhythms, sync up, and keep the vibe alive.

Hey, love's a journey, not a destination. Remember to enjoy the ride and learn from every twist and turn! ♡ 📶 📖

## Resilience in Romance

**The Power of Bouncing Back:**
Heartbreaks, misunderstandings, or unreciprocated feelings can sting. But here's the tea: they're not the end, but a bend in your love journey. Emotions may run high, and nights may feel long, but with every dawn, there's a chance to start anew. Think of setbacks not as definitive endings, but as lessons you take into the next chapter. Your heart might hurt now, but it's also gathering strength for the love stories yet to be written.

**Understanding 'No': A Redirect, Not a Rejection:**
It's natural to feel deflated when someone says "No." But here's a fresh perspective: maybe it's not about you being inadequate, but about the universe signaling that there's a different path, a different story awaiting you. Every "No" you face isn't a verdict on your worth, but rather a signpost guiding

you to where you truly belong. For all you know, a much more meaningful "Yes" is just around the corner!

**The Emotional Landscape of 'Could-Have-Beens':**
Those moments of "almosts," those "what if" thoughts can feel like shadowy clouds over your emotional skyline. They're the bittersweet residues of romance that might leave you pondering on the endless possibilities. But remember, while it's natural to think about what might have been, it's also vital to realize the value of what is and what's yet to come. Your feelings are valid, and it's okay to mourn the might-have-beens, but the future holds countless more moments waiting to be seized.

Navigating the realm of romance isn't always a breezy summer afternoon. Sometimes it's a wintry night, where all seems cold and lost. But even then, remember, the warmth of spring isn't far. Emotions will ebb and flow; that's the nature of love. Through the highs and the lows, your heart learns, grows, and readies itself for the beautiful tales yet to unfold. 🐑 🌿 🐚

# Chapter 14: Money Matters - Your Guide to Financial Wisdom

## Banking Basics

### The ABCs of Banks:

Ah, banks. Those grand buildings or sometimes tiny nooks where so much magic (read: money stuff) happens. So, what's the real deal?

*Banks* are institutions that hold onto your money (yes, that precious allowance or birthday cash) and help you manage it. In return, they sometimes pay you interest for trusting them with your funds. They also provide loans to people, and that's another way they make money - by charging interest on those loans.

**Accounts and You:**
Ever heard of the saying, "Don't put all your eggs in one basket?" Well, with banks, you can choose which basket (or account) suits you best.

- *Savings Account:* The classic choice. It's where you store your money, earn some interest, and watch your savings grow like a plant in the sunshine.

- *Checking Account:* The everyday hero. Perfect for daily transactions, like buying that new book or paying for a movie ticket. No interest here, but you get a checkbook and an ATM card.

- *Fixed Deposits:* The long-term commitment. You leave a sum of money untouched for a while (say, a year or more), and in return, the bank pays you more interest than a regular savings account would. As of August 21, 2023, the average U.S. savings account has an interest rate of 0.43%, as stated by the FDIC. Now, what's the real deal with this? If you park $100 in such a savings account, by the end of the year, you'll have an extra 43 cents. Not a fortune, but it's a start!

Remember, every bank has its own set of account types with varied features, so always read the fine print!

**Debit and Credit Cards:**
Alright, game time. Debit and credit cards look super similar, but they've got different superpowers.

- *Debit Card:* Think of it as a magic key to your bank account. Every time you swipe, you're using your own money. So, if there's no money in the account, the card won't work. It keeps things real!

- *Credit Card:* This one's a bit trickier. It's like the bank saying, "Hey, shop now and pay us later!" But remember, this isn't free money. You'll have to pay back what you spent, and if you delay, there'll be interest charges. As of September 11, 2023, credit cards come with an average interest rate of 28.02%, according to a report by Forbes Advisor. In human terms? If you splurge with $100 on your card and don't pay off the balance for an entire year, you're going to owe an extra $28.02 just in interest. So, wield this power wisely!

In both cases, guard your card details. Always. Because in the wrong hands, they can lead to some serious financial oopsies.

## Currency Conundrums

**Around the World in Different Currencies:**
Ever wondered why your friend in Japan pays for stuff in Yen and your buddy in England uses Pounds? Welcome to the world of diverse currencies! Each country (or group of countries) has its own currency, a kind of money they use.
**USD (U.S. Dollar):** The superstar of global trade.
**EUR (Euro):** Used by 19 of the 27 European Union countries. Talk about teamwork!
**JPY (Japanese Yen):** Spend these in Tokyo for all things cool.
**GBP (British Pound Sterling):** The Brits' pride and one of the world's oldest currencies still in use.

**Exchange Rate Magic:** This is the rate at which one currency can be swapped for another. It's how you figure out how many

Euros your Dollar can buy. These rates fluctuate based on various factors like economies' health, political stability, and global events. Some folks even make money by trading currencies, buying when they're "cheap" and selling when their value goes up. It's a bit like the stock market but with currencies!

# Cryptocurrency: 🚀 What's the Buzz?

At its core, cryptocurrency is a type of digital or virtual money. Unlike the dollars or euros you might hold in your hand or keep in a bank, cryptocurrency exists purely online. Imagine having a type of money that's entirely powered by computers all over the world.

## 🌐 The Birth of Cryptocurrency: A Revolutionary Idea

The idea behind cryptocurrency is to have a currency free from central banks or governments. The story began in 2008 with someone (or possibly a group) named Satoshi Nakamoto. They introduced the world to Bitcoin, the very first cryptocurrency. The main idea? Create a decentralized currency that lets people make transactions without needing banks or middlemen.

## ☑ The Superstars of the Crypto World

While Bitcoin was the pioneer, it's not the only player. Here are some of the big names:
**Bitcoin (BTC)**: The OG (Original Gangster) of crypto.
**Ethereum (ETH)**: Not just a currency, but a platform that lets developers create apps on its blockchain.

**Ripple (XRP)**: Known for its digital payment protocol more than its cryptocurrency.

**Litecoin (LTC)**: Created as the "silver" to Bitcoin's "gold".

## 🏦 Pros of Cryptocurrency:

1. **Decentralization**: No government or bank controls it.
2. **Transparency**: All transactions are recorded on a public ledger called the blockchain.
3. **Potential for Growth**: Some early investors in cryptocurrencies saw their values skyrocket.

## ☁ Cons of Cryptocurrency:

1. **Volatility**: Crypto prices can swing wildly in short amounts of time.
2. **Lack of Understanding**: Not everyone gets it, and that can make its future uncertain.
3. **Potential for Loss**: If you lose access to your crypto wallet, you can't get your money back.

## 💡 Final Thoughts:

Cryptocurrency is an exciting and ever-evolving world. If you ever consider diving in, make sure you do your research and understand the risks. It's a bit like the wild west of the digital age, full of opportunity, but with its share of challenges too!

Remember, cryptocurrency, like all investments, comes with risks. Always educate yourself and consult with trusted individuals before making financial decisions.

# *Decoding Credits*

## Investment or Debt?: When Is Taking a Loan a Good Idea?

We often hear about loans as being 'debt', which can sound pretty scary. But not all debt is bad! Sometimes, borrowing money can be an investment for your future. The trick is to differentiate between *good debt* and *bad debt*.

### ⊚ Good Debt:

This is when you borrow money that'll benefit you in the long run. It might be a college loan that helps you get a better-paying job after you graduate, or a business loan to kickstart your startup dream.

### ⃠ Bad Debt:

This is when the things you're borrowing for lose value quickly or aren't essential. Think of borrowing money to buy the latest smartphone or designer clothes. They're cool to have but might not be worth the long-term cost of the loan.

💧 **Tip**: Always ask yourself: "Will this loan improve my future, or is it just for a short-term desire?"

## College Loans - An Investment in You.

Heading to college is a significant step, filled with the promise of new experiences, profound learning, and potentially, a pathway to your dream job. But it's also a pricey proposition, hence the consideration of college loans.

## 💡 Understanding the Investment:

When you take a loan for college, you're essentially betting on yourself. The hope? That the education you receive will eventually lead to better job opportunities and a comfortable income to repay that loan.

## 😊 Assessing the Decision:

Before committing to college loans, it's crucial to introspect:

**Financial Reward:** Will your intended degree lead to well-paying jobs? Some fields have higher earning potentials which can make loan repayment smoother.

**Passion Pursuit:** Some fields might not promise the highest salaries, but if it's what you're passionate about, it can be worth it. Just ensure you understand the balance between following your heart and managing future debts.

**Alternative Paths:** Scholarships, grants, or part-time jobs can be ways to mitigate the amount you need to borrow. Every little bit helps!

## 🔲 Different Routes to Success:

It's essential to remember that college is just one of many paths to success. Many successful individuals have forged their unique journeys without a traditional college degree. In such cases, diving into a significant amount of debt via college loans might not be the wisest choice. Whether it's pursuing vocational training, starting an apprenticeship, or venturing into entrepreneurship, the world is brimming with opportunities. Assess if college aligns with your personal and professional goals.

🔥 **Tip:** College is about more than just a potential paycheck. It's about personal growth, networking, and following passions. However, always be financially savvy and consider all paths before making decisions that come with long-term financial commitments.

In today's dynamic world, it's pivotal to understand that there are multiple avenues to achieve your dreams. Equip yourself with information, stay adaptable, and carve your unique path.

## From Teen to Employee: Navigating U.S. Work Regulations

### Why the Restrictions?: Navigating Age-Related Work Rules

The U.S. has set regulations about when and how teens can work. Let's break it down:

1. **Age 14-15**:
   **Work Hours**: Outside of school hours, these teens can work up to 3 hours on school days, 8 hours on non-school days, and a maximum of 18 hours per week during school weeks. During non-school weeks, they can work up to 40 hours. They can't work before 7 a.m. or after 7 p.m., but the evening limit extends to 9 p.m. from June 1 to Labor Day.
   **Job Types**: They're restricted to certain jobs, often excluding manufacturing, mining, and most jobs in places like factories or warehouses to prioritize safety.

2. **Age 16-17**:
   **Work Hours**: No federal limitations on hours, but some states might have their own rules.

**Job Types**: These teens can take on a wider range of jobs, but anything deemed hazardous by the Secretary of Labor is off-limits.

3. **Age 18 and up**: Once you hit 18, you're generally considered an adult in the eyes of employment law. This means you can work any job for any hours.

🔥 **Tip**: Always check the regulations in your specific state, as some states may have more stringent rules than federal guidelines.

## Mind Over Age: The Sky's the Limit with Ambition

Yes, there are restrictions, but the digital world offers an expansive playground for the young and ambitious:

1. **Digital Freedom**: If you have a computer and internet access, age barriers start to blur. Many teens are capitalizing on e-commerce, blogging, content creation, and even app development.

2. **Learning and Adaptability**: While older folks boast experience, teens often bring adaptability and a quick learning curve—key assets in today's fast-paced digital realm.

3. **Real-life Success Stories**: Take someone like Ben Pasternak, an entrepreneur who began his journey at 15. He's not an outlier; numerous teens, especially in the USA, are leveraging the digital age to make their mark.

🔥 **Tip**: Don't let age deter you. With the right mindset and resources, you can achieve your entrepreneurial dreams, even as a teen!

With knowledge of the laws and a dash of determination, there's no stopping what you can accomplish. Always stay informed, and remember, age is just a number when it comes to potential!

## *Time for Challenge!*

### 🎇 Exercise #1: "Side Hustle Brainstorm Party" 🎇

**Goal:** Gather friends and brainstorm cool and creative ways to earn money.

**Step 1:** Host a fun brainstorm session (in-person or virtually) with snacks, music, and a relaxed vibe.
**Step 2:** Everyone pitches their unique earning ideas — from crafting and selling, starting a YouTube channel, to offering local services like lawn mowing or dog walking.
**Step 3:** Choose the top three most exciting and feasible ideas and discuss the first steps to implement them.

### 🎇 Exercise #2: "Skill Swap Fair" 🎇

**Goal:** Exchange skills with peers to bolster your money-making abilities.

**Step 1:** Identify a skill you're good at, like photography, writing, graphic design, or coding.

**Step 2:** Organize a day where friends or classmates can "swap" teaching skills. Someone might teach you basic guitar chords, while you offer a lesson on effective Instagram photography.

**Step 3:** With your new skill in hand, explore ways to monetize it. For instance, if you've learned basic guitar, consider street performing or offering beginner lessons.

### 🎇 Exercise #3: "Pop-Up Enterprise Day" 🎇

**Goal:** Test your entrepreneurial spirit with a one-day business.

**Step 1:** Choose a product or service you can offer for one day. This could be a lemonade stand, car wash service, a pop-up thrift store, or a baked goods sale.

**Step 2:** Plan the logistics — where you'll set up, how you'll promote it (maybe a fun social media campaign?), and what you'll need in terms of supplies.

**Step 3:** At the end of the day, evaluate the experience. How much did you earn? What went well, and what could be improved? It's a fun way to get hands-on business experience.

# 10 Fun Ways to Make Money: simple ideas that can turn into cash in a few days with ChatGPT.

### 1. Custom Bedtime Stories for Kids 🌙
**Step-by-Step**:
  1. Ask parents/kids about the child's favorite things.
  2. Use ChatGPT: "Create a story about a bunny named Benji who goes to a chocolate mountain."
  3. Add personal touches!
**Sell it**: Post on community boards, Facebook groups, or local newsletters.
**Example**: "Benji the bunny hopped excitedly towards the towering chocolate mountain, where every rock was a candy..."
🍫 **Tip**: Offer "story bundles" for a week's worth of bedtime tales!

### 2. Homework Helper 🎓
**Step-by-Step**:
  1. Get a list of topics students in your school struggle with.
  2. Use ChatGPT: "Explain the water cycle for 6th graders."
  3. Create easy-to-follow notes or doodles.
**Sell it**: Advertise in school groups or chat groups, community boards or tutoring platforms.
**Example**: "The water cycle is like Earth's way of recycling water! It goes from clouds to rain to rivers and back up!"
🍫 **Tip**: Offer a buddy discount – two sessions for a slightly reduced price per session.

### 3. Unique Greeting Cards 💝
**Step-by-Step**:
  1. Choose popular occasions like birthdays or anniversaries.
  2. Use ChatGPT: "Write a birthday message for a soccer-loving teen."
  3. Design it using free tools like Canva.

**Sell it**: Print and sell at school events and local markets, or go digital on Etsy or social media! .

**Example**: "Kick off another awesome year, champ! Happy Birthday!"

🎖 **Tip**: Custom messages for extra special occasions can fetch a premium! Offer personalized handcrafted designs.

## 4. Virtual Travel Guide 🌐
**Step-by-Step**:
1. Pick popular teen vacation spots.
2. Use ChatGPT: "List cool places for teens in Tokyo."
3. Make a snazzy PDF guide.

**Sell it**: Advertise on travel forums or family FB groups, on travel blogs, local community forums, or travel agencies.

**Example**: "1. Akihabara: Gamer's paradise! 🎮 2. Takeshita Street: Shop till you drop! 🛍"

🎖 **Tip**: Upsell with personalized daily itineraries.

## 5. Custom Role-Playing Game Scenarios 🎲
**Step-by-Step**:
1. Understand the game setting.
2. Use ChatGPT: "Design a quest for a magic forest."
3. Polish it up, make it exciting!

**Sell it**: On RPG forums, Discord servers, or with gaming buddies.

**Example**: "Quest: Retrieve the Enchanted Acorn from the Elder Tree, but beware the mischievous forest sprites!"

🎖 **Tip**: Bundle scenarios into a 'game pack' for more cash!

## 6. Brand Name and Slogan Generator 💡
**Step-by-Step**:
1. Get to know a startup's vibe.
2. Use ChatGPT: "Name for a vintage clothing shop."
3. Add your creative twist!

**Sell it**: Offer services on platforms like Fiverr or to local businesses.

**Example**: "RetroThreads: Where the Past Meets Present!"

🏵 **Tip**: Premium pricing for name + logo combos!

## 7. Custom Quizzes and Trivia 🤭
**Step-by-Step**:
1. Choose a fun theme like '90s cartoons.
2. Use ChatGPT: "Trivia questions on '90s cartoons."
3. Create a cool interactive quiz using Google Forms.

**Sell it**: Host quiz nights in community centers or online!
Organize trivia nights at cafes or online Zoom parties!
**Example**: "Which '90s cartoon features a wallaby named
Rocko? A) Doug B) Rocko's Modern Life"

🏵 **Tip**: Charge teams to enter your quiz night and offer a prize
for the winner!

## 8. DIY Guides & How-Tos ✂
**Step-by-Step**:
1. Find a fun DIY, like making friendship bracelets.
2. Use ChatGPT: "Steps to create a beaded friendship
bracelet."
3. Make it visually appealing!

**Sell it**: At craft fairs, online shops, or weekend workshops.
**Example**: "1. Choose your fav beads. 2. Thread 'em. 3. Knot
and wear!"

🏵 **Tip**: Offer DIY kits with materials for a complete crafting
experience.

## 9. Personalized Poetry on Demand 🏵
**Step-by-Step**:
1. Gather themes or emotions.
2. Use ChatGPT: "Write a poem about summer nights."
3. Add some personal touches.

**Sell it**: At local events, online platforms, or cafes during poetry
readings..
**Example**: "Under the blanket of stars, summer whispers tales
of far..."

🏵 **Tip**: Offer framed versions for a higher price!

## 10. Daily Fun Fact Service 🌐
**Step-by-Step**:
1. Choose categories like 'Animals' or 'Space.'
2. Use ChatGPT: "Fun fact about marsupials."
3. Share it with cool graphics!

**Sell it**: A subscription service – daily tidbits to enlighten and entertain!

**Example**: "Did you know? Koalas have fingerprints similar to humans!"

# Chapter 15: Navigating Your Future: Finding Your Ideal Career.

## Profession Types

1. **People-centric Professions** (e.g., Sales, Counseling, Teaching, Public Relations, Nursing)
   - *Skills Needed*: Strong interpersonal skills, empathy, patience, communication.
   - *Pros*: Fulfilling interactions, direct impact on people, relationship building.
   - *Cons*: Emotionally taxing, demands constant interpersonal interactions.

2. **Data-driven Professions** (e.g., Data Analysis, Accounting, Actuarial Science, Market Research)
   - *Skills Needed*: Analytical thinking, attention to detail, logical reasoning.
   - *Pros*: Structured tasks, tangible results, high demand in many industries.
   - *Cons*: Repetitive, continuous adaptation to evolving tools and technologies.

3. **Nature-related Professions** (e.g., Botany, Environmental Engineering, Wildlife Photography, Forestry)
   - *Skills Needed*: Appreciation for nature, observational skills, adaptability.
   - *Pros*: Contribution to conserving the environment, often outdoors, diverse daily tasks.
   - *Cons*: Physically demanding, exposure to elements, irregular hours.

4. **Creative Arts Professions** (e.g., Graphic Design, Writing, Film Production, Music Composition)
   - *Skills Needed*: Creativity, visualization, adaptability, technical proficiency in chosen medium.
   - *Pros*: Freedom of expression, potential for unique projects, emotional fulfilment.

- *Cons*: Highly competitive, subjective evaluations, inconsistent work opportunities.


5. **Technical & Engineering Professions** (e.g., Hardware Development, Mechanical Engineering, Architecture)
   - *Skills Needed*: Problem-solving, precision, mathematical and logical reasoning.
   - *Pros*: High demand, well-compensated, continuous learning opportunities.
   - *Cons*: Often desk-bound, long hours, rapid technological changes

6. **Physical & Skill-based Professions** (e.g., Athletics, Carpentry, Culinary Arts, Dance)
   - *Skills Needed*: Physical fitness, hand-eye coordination, precision, dedication.
   - *Pros*: Tangible outcomes, potential for recognition, offers physical activity.
   - *Cons*: Physically taxing, potential for injury, may have a shorter career span.

These categories encompass a broad spectrum of professions. It's essential to understand that many careers overlap between categories, and one's interests and skills can lead to success in multiple areas. The idea is to find where your passion meets a need in the world.

# Test yourself!

## 1. People-centric Professions

*Exercise*: Role-playing scenario with a friend where one acts as a counsellor and the other as a client facing a challenge.

*Prompts*:
- Name a time when you helped someone through a tough situation.
- What emotions do you feel when you positively impact someone's life?
- Which people-centric jobs sound appealing to you, and why?

## 2. Data-driven Professions

*Exercise*: Analyse a small set of fictional data (like sales of different products over a month) and identify patterns or trends.

*Prompts*:
- When you think about numbers or data, what emotions come to mind?
- Describe a situation where you successfully used logic to solve a problem.
- Which aspects of data analysis excite you the most?

## 3. Nature-related Professions

*Exercise*: Take a walk in nature and journal about the different species of plants or animals you encounter.

*Prompts*:
- Describe a moment when you felt connected to nature.
- If you could work outdoors, where would your ideal location be?
- What nature-related issues are you most passionate about addressing?

## 4. Creative Arts Professions

*Exercise*: Create a quick piece of art or story, given a prompt or theme. It could be a drawing, poem, or a short film clip.

*Prompts*:
- Think about a time your creativity surprised you. What did you create?
- What medium (writing, painting, film) do you feel most drawn to?
- Describe a piece of art that deeply moved you. Why did it have that effect?

## 5. Technical & Engineering Professions

*Exercise*: Build a simple structure using LEGO or any available materials that can hold a small weight.

*Prompts*:
- Describe a problem you faced and how you approached solving it step by step.
- What kind of technology or engineering feats make you curious about how they work?
- Think about a gadget or app idea that could solve a daily problem you face.

## 6. Physical & Skill-based Professions

*Exercise*: Choose a simple skill (like juggling, basic cooking recipe, or a dance step) and practice it.

*Prompts*:
- When was the last time you felt accomplished by mastering a physical skill or task?
- Which physical activities give you the most joy or satisfaction?
- If you could learn one new physical skill right now, what would it be?

These exercises are designed to encourage introspection, helping you align interests and passions with potential career paths. Remember, the goal isn't to pigeonhole oneself into one category but to explore and discover where one's joy and skills meet the world's needs.

# Taking the First Steps Toward Career Choice

After having a bit of introspection and understanding your inclinations from the previous exercises, you might have some career paths in mind. So, how do you start turning those ideas into reality? Let's break it down.

## 1. Understanding Work Terminology

**Job**: This is a specific position of employment in an organization or company where you do particular tasks in exchange for money, benefits, or other compensation. It's often short-term and based on necessity rather than passion.

**Career**: This is a long-term professional journey you might decide upon. It's a series of connected employment opportunities, where you build up skills at earlier employment opportunities to move you into higher paying and higher prestige employment opportunities later on.

**Calling**: This is work that you feel naturally drawn to. It's when what you do aligns so closely with who you are that it doesn't feel like work. It's based on passion and can intersect with a career or job.

## 2. Testing the Waters with Real-Life Experience

Before you set your heart on a specific career path, it's crucial to get a taste of what the work is really like. Here's how:

**Internships**: These are often short-term, sometimes paid (or unpaid) positions that allow you to observe and participate in daily operations of a field you're interested in. It's like test-driving a career.

**Part-time Jobs**: Even if it's not directly related to your dream career, part-time jobs can teach you invaluable skills like time management, customer service, and teamwork.

**Volunteer Opportunities**: Not only do you get to give back to the community, but volunteering can also give you a good feel for certain professions. For instance, if you're considering a career in veterinary medicine, volunteering at an animal shelter could provide some insights.

## 3. Extracurricular Activities as a Career Mirror

The clubs, sports, and activities you participate in during your school years can often be a mirror reflecting your future career interests.

- Are you in the debate club? Perhaps you have a knack for public speaking and might excel in professions like law or public relations.

- If you're the president of your school's environment club, maybe a career in environmental science or policy-making is in your future.

## 4. Linking Insights to Action

Now, remember the insights you gained from the previous exercise? It's time to test them:

- If you felt drawn to **People-centric Professions** and you enjoyed role-playing as a counselor, consider volunteering at a helpline or shadowing professionals in fields like teaching or counseling.

- Drawn towards **Creative Arts**? Join or start a school newspaper, yearbook committee, or drama club.

- For those inclined towards **Technical & Engineering Professions**, join a robotics club, or take additional computer classes.

It's essential to remember that choosing a career is a journey, not a destination. Your interests may evolve, and that's okay. The key is to remain curious, open-minded, and proactive in seeking opportunities to learn and grow.

# *Chapter 16: Ride the Rollercoaster of Life!*

## 1. Control Freaks Beware! 🎮

Hey, guess what? We can't control everything, and that's totally okay! Embrace the unpredictability. The best video games are those with surprise twists, right?

## 2. Dive into the Unknown 🌊

Feel stuck? Dive into new waters! Life's all about trying new levels, exploring uncharted territories, and unlocking hidden achievements. Don't just wait on the shore; dive in and find your treasures.

## 3. Oops, I Did It Again! 👾

Made a mistake? Cool, that's a bonus learning level! Own up, level up, and gear up for the next adventure. Every choice, good or bad, is a step towards leveling up in the game of life.

### 4. Surprise! Life's Got Goodies! 🎁

Sometimes when you're expecting a troll, life throws you a power-up! Trust the journey. Remember: the best goodies often pop up when you least expect them.

### *Challenge: "Positive Vibes Playlist"* 🎇

**Step 1:** Create a new playlist titled "Positive Vibes."
**Step 2:** Throughout the week, add songs that uplift you or bring back happy memories.
**Step 3:** Whenever you're feeling down or just need a boost, press play. Let the music elevate your spirit. Bonus: Share your playlist with friends and spread the joy!

Made in the USA
Las Vegas, NV
17 December 2024

14564024R00069